Aunt Ester's Children Redeemed

Aunt Ester's Children Redeemed

Journeys to Freedom in August Wilson's Ten Plays
of Twentieth-Century Black America

Riley Keene Temple

CASCADE *Books* · Eugene, Oregon

AUNT ESTER'S CHILDREN REDEEMED
Journeys to Freedom in August Wilson's Ten Plays
of Twentieth-Century Black America

Cascade Books
An Imprint of Wipf and Stock Publishers
199 W. 8th Ave., Suite 3
Eugene, OR 97401

www.wipfandstock.com

PAPERBACK ISBN: 978-1-4982-3780-2
HARDCOVER ISBN: 978-1-4982-3782-6
EBOOK ISBN: 978-1-4982-3781-9

Cataloguing-in-Publication data:

Names: Temple, Riley Keene.

Title: Aunt Ester's children redeemed : journeys to freedom in August Wilson's ten plays of twentieth-century black America / Riley Keene Temple.

Description: Eugene, OR : Cascade Books, 2017 | Includes bibliographical references.

Identifiers: ISBN 978-1-4982-3780-2 (paperback) | ISBN 978-1-4982-3782-6 (hardcover) | ISBN 978-1-4982-3781-9 (ebook)

Subjects: LSCH: Wilson, August—Criticism and interpretation.

Classification: PS3573.I45677 Z90 2017 (print) | PS3573.I45677 Z90 (ebook)

Manufactured in the U.S.A.   01/24/17

To my parents
David and Helen

Contents

Introduction | vii

I   *Gem of the Ocean*: Aunt Ester and 1839 Wylie Avenue | 1

II   I'm Standing Now! Herald Loomis Redeemed:
Joe Turner's Come and Gone | 13

III   God Hate Niggers: The Tragedy of *Ma Rainey's
Black Bottom* | 25

IV   Mark That Day Down: *The Piano Lesson* | 37

V   They Came Down Out the Sky: Finding Redemption
in *Seven Guitars* | 49

VI   Banish Them with Forgiveness: *Fences* | 61

VII   *Two Trains Running* | 75

VIII   Paying Redemption's Dues: *Jitney* | 87

IX   Danger—All About Them—Danger: *King Hedley II* | 95

X   All of Aunt Ester's Children Redeemed: *Radio Golf* | 109

Epilogue | 119

Bibliography | 125

Acknowledgments | 129

Introduction

1984. A SOLITARY MID-WEEK escape to Manhattan, and an indulgent over-night stay in a luxurious Upper East Side hotel, would be mere accessories to the main event—a visit to the theater—to Broadway's Cort Theater this time—to experience first-hand the source of this frisson that was August Wilson. He had a new play, fresh from the Yale Repertory Theater, and directed by its artistic director and the Drama School's venerable Dean, Lloyd Richards.[1] The play was *Ma Rainey's Black Bottom*. And it was that night that I began my intellectual and emotional journey with August Wilson.

I was not prepared for the apparent event that was the evening. There were luminati everywhere, although it was not opening night nor was it a benefit performance. It was well into the run. The point is that August Wilson had already begun to take on iconic status in literary circles in black America—as someone we needed to listen to and learn from. My seat was on the right aisle, center orchestra section, and halfway back. Perfect. I arrived early, as always. I looked up, and noticed the unmistakable and distinctive silhouette and gait of the then (and now late) Chicago Mayor, Harold Washington. The setting of the play was Chicago, after all.[2] And then at the intermission I suddenly noticed that I was standing next to the

1. A generation before, Lloyd Richards had given directorial life to Lorraine Hansberry's, *A Raisin in the Sun* (1959). It would be the first time a play written by a black woman would be performed on Broadway.

2. That it was Chicago would prove unique in the Ten Play Cycle. All of the others take place in the Hill District of Pittsburgh.

great man of letters (now late), James Baldwin. They, like me, had come to pay homage. It was a new voice. August Wilson had a voice.

Ma Rainey was riveting—even harsh for proud ethnic or devout sensibilities.[3] I did not grasp at the time the metaphor of Ma Rainey's need to control every detail as a stand-in for her essential dignity—her being—her self. What I do recall is its poetry and its unrelenting power and dramatic tension. Nor could I ever forget the young, brash trumpeter's ghastly verbal assaults hurled at God, and the audible gasps and even screams from the audience in response. The cast was brilliant. There was, of course, Theresa Merritt as Ma, but also a breakthrough performance by a young Charles Dutton as Levee. It was this role that would make him a fixture among the August Wilson cadre of actors. It would also place him unimpeachably among the finest actors in English-speaking theater. Despite the tragic end, the loud and foolish arguments and senseless violence—all metaphors for the struggles and challenges for wholeness and meaning—I did not experience *Ma Rainey* as an exploration of theological territory. Nor did I quite yet see the centrality, the essence of the song, the blues, as the unifying theme—not only in this play, but also in finding who we are. Few people did, I suspect. I would have to mature a bit, and see (and read) more Wilson before any themes of redemption would occur to me.

Then in 1987 came *Fences*, with the heavyweight talent and voice of James Earl Jones in the lead as Troy, and a sublime Mary Alice as Rose.[4] Broadway's 46th Street Theater was its home after Yale. By this time the theater *cognoscenti* were all watching. The result: Jones and Alice both won lead-acting Tony Awards, and *Fences* won the Pulitzer Prize for drama. Jones was already established on stage and screen, but Mary Alice became (and remains) the female actor of choice when serious professional work and real talent are required. *Fences* launched the career of Courtney Vance who played Troy and Rose's son, Cory. My experience with *Fences* one Saturday matinee was that I left completely spent emotionally after Rose speaks—sings really—of her dreams and disappointments as she faces the unearthed and harsh truths of Troy's long-term unfaithfulness. She

3. It had become quite rare, for example, to hear black actors loudly and unapologetically cursing God, and to hear the casual and repeated use of "nigger" in dialogue.

4. Rumor had it that August Wilson was not pleased with Mary Alice as Rose. He apparently found her speech not lyrical enough, nor sufficiently expressive. Audiences and critics disagreed. She, in fact, spoke with a staccato-like way of delivery as Rose, and a somewhat peculiar flat disposition against Jones's explosive outbursts. But it worked wonderfully.

then closes the last moments of the play in the wideness of her mercy and forgiveness as she invites her son to forgive, as well, the dead Troy—his father—of his sins against him. Wilson's closing scenes in *Fences* are the greatness of epic poetry, of blues, of Blues Opera.

From the balcony of Arena Stage's Kreeger Theater in the autumn of 1987 I saw *Joe Turner's Come and Gone*, directed again by Lloyd Richards and in co-production with Arena on its way to a commercial run in New York. Unlike the last two, *Joe Turner* had a metaphysical core that forced the audience to suspend reality—dreams, visions, ghosts, and ancient African rituals. It was brilliantly poetic and visually stunning. For the first time in a Wilson drama (and not for the last), characters were required to address the tension—the coexistence—between their devotion to a God of the enslaver, and their own personal God to be fully redeemed by coming to terms with the spirits of the African ancestors. *Joe Turner* was also a "must see." Its cast included young actors such as Angela Bassett[5] and Delroy Lindo in nascent development. By this time, the August Wilson play had arrived as a standard of American drama. His work was now a solid part of the seasons of professional theaters throughout the country.[6]

With *The Piano Lesson*, Wilson won his second Pulitzer Prize for drama. He was also well on his way to completing a Century Cycle of Plays—a play for every decade of the 20th century. It was not a goal he set out to accomplish when he first drafted *Jitney* in 1977, and followed with a play called *Fullerton Street* set in 1941, nor when he submitted *Ma Rainey* to the Eugene O'Neill Playwrights Conference in Connecticut. But he realized that he had these plays, each set in a different decade, and he thought he would simply carry on. The idea of a different decade for each gave him a focus, and a purpose, and he did not have to guess at the source for the next idea.[7]

Never before in the history of American theater has there been such an epic focus on African-American culture and identity by one artist with such singularly astute and lyrical abilities. Wilson's poetic genius is on full display in the iteration of each decade, and each is a celebration of community—a community we regard as invaluable as Christians. He celebrates

5. Bassett was a 1987 graduate of the Yale School of Drama.

6. I eventually saw all of the plays, but not in New York. I often experienced them in fine noncommercial productions in Washington, Chicago, and Atlanta (once sitting beside Wilson, himself).

7. Sheppard, "August Wilson," 102.

black Americans as men and women of high purpose with a culture so rich and full as to sustain them in all areas of human endeavor. Wilson's characters are strong in faith and are "continually negotiating for a position, the high ground . . . from which they best shout an affirmation of the value and worth of their being in the face of a many million voice chorus that seeks to deafen and obliterate it."[8]

What are they? *Gem of the Ocean* (2003) set in 1904; *Joe Turner's Come and Gone* (1988) set in 1911; *Ma Rainey's Black Bottom* (1981–1985) set in 1927; *The Piano Lesson* (1990) set in 1936; *Seven Guitars* (1996) set in 1948; *Fences* (1986) set in 1957; *Two Trains Running* (1992) set in 1969; *Jitney* (1979) set in 1977; *King Hedley II* (2000) set in 1985; and *Radio Golf* (2007) set in 1997. With the exception of *Jitney*, all the others would find their way to the commercial landscape of Broadway, a peerless standard for a playwright of drama.[9]

And because of the sheer beauty and lofty significance of his work, great theater artists have clamored to be a part of the Wilson canon. The Cycle is important. It celebrates. It speaks about. It speaks to. It identifies. It saves. Yet the demands are too great for most actors, and only the most able and worthy qualify. The speeches, while nominally colloquial, are written by Wilson the poet, the man who loves the blues. The blues is what he hears. He infuses his dialogue with the rhythm and lyrics of the blues, transfers that to the page, to the stage and to the voice. Theresa Merritt, Phylicia Rashad, Leslie Uggams, Charles Dutton, Angela Bassett, Delroy Lindo, Reuben

8. Wilson, "Aunt Ester's Children: A Century on Stage," 28 and 30.

9. There is the one-actor play, *How I Learned What I Learned*, which was co-conceived by August Wilson and his dramaturge, Todd Kreidler, and performed by Wilson at the Seattle Rep in 2005. The play has never been published, but this writer has had access to its unpublished script. In it Wilson shares the memories and influences of the people and ideas from his earlier years in Pittsburgh—those times that shaped him as a poet and playwright. For those who know his canon it is a poignant time spent with the artist, for we see the beginnings of characters, principles, forces, and poetry that resonate throughout the Century Cycle. "It's the principle of the thing," says August Wilson. Thus we see the man in *Gem*, Garrett Brown, who would rather drown than live and be falsely accused of stealing a bag of nails; *Ma Rainey*, who would rather unreasonably hold up the works of recording than to have her essential dignity minimized; Troy Maxson in *Fences* who would rather his son keep a grocery store job than to be reduced in sports because of color; Hambone in *Two Trains* who would take nothing less than what he was promised for a job well-done; or King Hedley who would seek to murder a second time in revenge for an alleged wrongful death. We also meet the colorful characters that emerge as those who exist in their own reality, such as Solly Two Kings (*Gem*), or Gabe (*Fences*), and Elder Joe Barlow (*Radio Golf*). *How I Learned* is an important, if not essential, accompaniment to the Century Cycle.

Santiago Hudson, Lawrence Fishburne, Kenny Leon, Samuel Jackson, Latasha Richardson Jackson, Mary Alice, James Earl Jones, Viola Davis, Denzel Washington, Paul Butler, Stephen McKinley Henderson, Courtney Vance, Anthony Chisholm, Brian Stokes Mitchell, the late Roscoe Lee Browne, S. Epatha Merkerson, and Alfre Woodard. They all bear witness to his "songs" of the spoken word. The list of others well known, but unable to withstand the artistic demands is longer, much longer.

This roll call of names is crucial, for it demonstrates the impact that this cycle has had on the artistic legacy in the creative world that is black America. The names have, in turn, brought to the theater thousands of people who may have never heard of August Wilson, yet who became devotees because they were attracted by the notion of seeing a live performance by one of these artists. They then experienced the community, the sanctuary, the sacred spaces, the worship experience, the celebration, the power of redemption, the higher ground that is the man and his creative genius.

What Rings Theological in Wilson's Century Cycle?

I took a degree in theology from an Episcopal Seminary and spent a considerable amount of effort in the study of Systematic Theology. And of course, one of the core tenets of Christian doctrine is that of the Trinity—the one in three—Father, Son, and Holy Spirit. One of the critical steps in the analysis of this Trinitarian mystery is that God "begat" his son, Jesus Christ, to take on human form—the Incarnation. What is this notion of begetting? Are there any worldly concepts to help in our understanding? Of course, I happened upon the artist, specifically, the novelist or playwright who creates characters—actually begets them. I recalled a one-day undergraduate seminar I had many years before with Ralph Ellison, author of the iconic and epic novel, *Invisible Man*.[10] I was among a small group of eager, besotted and pretentious sophomores who peppered this great writer with questions about his complex characters and their motivations. His patience, but never his graciousness, wearing thin, Ellison took a long draw from his cigarette (we were all smoking then—it was 1969) and said that our interpretations of what motivates his characters and what their actions might mean were as valid as his—that although he created them, that they are him and he they [he begat them?]—they nonetheless have their own motivations and urges

10. Random House, 1952.

and personalities and take on a personality all their own in the mind of each reader who encounters them.[11] The characters are indistinguishable from the creator, but fully creatures of free will, and can be engaged—should be engaged—must be engaged separately from the creator who begat them.

Thus, in Systematics I reflected again upon a writer's created world in August Wilson's comments about his characters and how they take over and speak to him, and how he then simply follows up. He does not question what he hears; he simply writes it down. It "comes from another place."[12] I began to examine Wilson's relationship as father and creator of his world of characters and circumstance, his identification with Aunt Ester (the Incarnate) and his and her spirit that live on to redeem and to sustain those who seek them. The artists-creators and the characters to which they give life cannot be separated—they are one and the same—a part of the artist's captured dreams and visions.

Of course, every writer of fiction creates a world that makes him or her a *god of creation*. But before one can become an artist, one must first *be*. It is "being" in all of its forms and definitions that gives the artist such a sense of self that is needed for the task of creation. Of his characters Wilson writes, "They're my partners, my friends . . . all the characters are part of *me* . . . they're all *me* . . . all this is made up out of myself"[13] (emphasis added).

I was then reminded of an idea of theologian John Zizioulas's that, "The truth of history lies in . . . created existence (since all beings are the willed realizations of God's love)."[14] Wilson has made known characters out of his love for them, and for his people.

I then played around with the Wilsonian world as Trinitarian, employing Aunt Ester, his favorite character, who makes her first appearance in *Gem of the Ocean*. She is over 300 years old—designed to be as old as the number of years that blacks have been on American soil. She is the repository, the embodiment, of the entire black experience in America—its wisdom and culture, traditions, philosophy, folkways, habits and hobbies.[15] Wilson is part of that story. She is his story. He created it. He claims it. She

11. I did not, could not, take it all in at that moment, that day, or for many years hence. I am still informed by it today—its import ever revelatory. Yet, I knew that I had experienced an epiphany about the process of creation, and the relationship of a creator (a writer) to his creation—the characters, the places, and the narrative.

12. Shannon, "August Wilson Explains His Dramatic Vision: An Interview," 141.

13. Moyers, "August Wilson: Playwright."

14. Zizioulas, *Being As Communion*, 98.

15. See Pettengill, "The Historical Perspective: An Interview with August Wilson."

is his autobiography—all three hundred plus years of it. She is August Wilson. She is the incarnation in his world. There are not two consciousnesses; "there is only one real consciousness."[16] She is a redeemer of souls; she is resurrected in *King Hedley II*, and continues to live on in spirit to redeem in *Radio Golf*.[17]

My theological interest in Wilson piqued, I began this exploration in earnest, eschewing the Trinitarian Doctrine, but getting closer to Wilson's heartbeat, I found more than ample texture and richness in the ideas of redemption—redemption in poetry, in sound, in rhythm, in blues, in history, memory and identity and in song. Wilson's created world of characters is redeemed through re-collected memory and search for identity—a search upheld by God, their God, the spirit and wisdom of a people. Consider Wilson's assessment of his people's status, and as a starting point—the panoply—the full landscape to take in as we begin this journey:

> They were brought across an ocean, chained in the hulls of 350-ton vessels. In the southern part of the United States, they were made to labor in the vast agricultural plantations. They made do without surnames and lived in dirt-floor cabins. They labored without pay. They were bought and sold and traded for money and gold and diamonds and molasses and horses and cows. They were fed the barest of subsistence diets. When they tried to escape, they were tracked down by men on horseback. They existed as an appendage to the body of society. They had no moral personality and no moral status in civic or church law . . . After 200-odd years, as a political expediency, they were granted freedom from being the property of other men. During the next hundred years they were disenfranchised, their houses were burned, they were hung from trees, forced into separate and inferior houses, schools and public facilities. They were granted status in law and denied it in practice.[18]

Wilson's poetic and profound summation of the tragic story of the African in America would serve as the point of departure for imagining his people without a clear sense of just who they might be. After generations of being torn asunder from culture and tradition, and out of sheer necessity of

16. Rahner, *The Trinity*, 107.

17. I am quite sure that my Trinitarian theory lacked the requisite coherence of great scholarship, but it was fun play. My Systematics professor, the Rev. Dr. Kate Sonderegger, was ever encouraging, gracious and tolerant. May she be forever blessed.

18. A. Wilson, "Aunt Ester's Children . . . " *American Theatre* (November 2005).

having to craft and carve and knit together what might be the remnants of what seems vaguely familiar, what renews, what inspires, what gives hope, and what comforts, there is inevitably a sense of who—an identity—a culture, tradition, belief.

Slaves in colonial America were not always subject to the Christian conversion impulses of their owners.[19] Conversions did happen, of course, but gained momentum especially during what is called the Great Protestant Awakening. The Methodists and the Presbyterians and the Baptists all set a standard of worship distinctly different from the staid and prim Anglican Church. And the preaching was far more evangelical, with clergy taken to preaching the Gospel not always inside the church buildings, but in the fields and along the highways. Charismatic sermonizers began to make noise about the evils of slavery, but such dissonant sounds died down rather quickly.

When in the Virginia of the 1770s people such as Robert Williams and Samuel Davies (who would eventually become the President of Princeton University) began to notice that the people they wanted as followers were also slave-owners, their anti-slavery messages disappeared. Instead, especially in Davies's case, they became slave-owners themselves, converted their slaves to Christianity and profited handsomely from their labor.[20] The converters taught, of course, that to be a good Christian you had to be a good slave. For some converters it may have been inconsequential, because they might have regarded slaves as being beyond the reach of the God/humanity relationship. Or even more simply, that an illiterate slave lacked the requisite mental capacity to grasp the philosophical concept of a deity.

19. See, e.g., Butler, *Awash in a Sea of Faith*. See also Levine, *Black Culture and Black Consciousness*. In this classic study, Levine argues that slaves, contrary to popular belief, did not abandon nor were completely cut off from their West African culture, heritage and various religious beliefs. Instead, those myriad societal cultures and norms were adapted into the slave culture and were essential tools to aid in survival of the slave experience. See as well Raboteau, *Slave Religion: The "Invisible Institution" in the Antebellum South*. Raboteau demonstrates that existent West African slave culture included, for many, beliefs in a God who was too exalted and mighty to be addressed by mere mortals, and thus they regularly worshipped smaller, multiple gods, who could intercede on their behalf. Such a belief structure made Roman Catholic conversion (especially in South America) quite common, given the Catholic notion of and reliance on the intercession of saints. It was the apparent segue into voodoo and spirits' possession of the body that unsettled the Catholic hierarchy.

20. Jewel L. Spangler writes brilliantly about the eighteenth-century religious "migration" on the issue of slavery. See *Virginians Reborn*.

Zora Neale Hurston had an answer. "They seemed to be staring at the dark. But their eyes were watching God."

What existed among the first Africans in America was a core belief in being surrounded by spirits that inhabit the animate and the inanimate world. And coexistent with that is this new concept of a God to help with this horrid and punishing world in which they found themselves. Theologian James Evans writes of blacks and their relationship with the Bible as, "Almost every [idea] of African-Americans was related to their condition of oppression and their desire for freedom. The hermeneutical perspective that they brought to the Bible was inseparable from their determination to live as full human beings in the presence of God."[21] It was a god of liberation they heard. It was a god that would not only bring them the hope of deliverance, but who would also help them to discover themselves, help their children, and their children after them to understand the foundation of their strength. They would understand—comprehend fully in the best sense—who and what have made them a *free* people in the purest sense, and would deliver them to a free place.

It is this coexistent Christian and African mysticism and spirituality that August Wilson explores. In his peoples' pilgrimages to reconstitute their selves rent asunder by America's mayhem, Wilson creates his most intriguing characters with feet and with language straddling the two realms—in poetry that sings the blues and carries the hope of the spirituals, in customs that dance the Juba after Sunday services while calling upon the Holy Ghost,[22] or while taking a mystical journey to the floor of the mid-Atlantic Ocean where a ship bearing manacled slaves sank generations before, and finding the mythical biblical city with twelve gates[23] as a means of redemption and finding freedom at long last—having a "soul washed."[24] There are others so wounded by a Christian God of the enslavers that only a time of complete conversion, baptism, rejection, or even sacrifice and resurrection can make them whole again.[25] How does Wilson structure a world for such wounded souls? What is the language he assigns to them and what does he bring to them as their salvation? His inspired

21. Evans, *We Have Been Believers*, 40.

22. *Joe Turner's Come and Gone.*

23. Rev 21:21.

24. *Gem of the Ocean.*

25. See, e.g., Levee in *Ma Rainey*, Herald Loomis in *Joe Turner*, Floyd in *Seven Guitars*, King in *King Hedley II.*

and collective response is Aunt Ester—she has the embodied wisdom and the knowledge to guide Wilson's created world down the redemption's road. This absorption of multiple cultural and spiritual traditions is a necessary aspect of the Wilson world, as it has been for the black world in which he lived. Poet Margaret Walker:

> We have been believers believing in the black gods of an old
>   land, believing in the secrets of the seeress and the
>   magic of the charmers and the power of the devil's evil
>   ones.
>
> And in the white gods of a new land we have been believers
>   believing in the mercy of our masters and the beauty of
>   our brothers, believing in the conjure of the humble
>   and the faithful and the pure.[26]

Walker, with the keen edge of the satirist's knife, slices through the notion that there is as much reason to believe in the white gods of the new land as there is reason to trust in the mercy of the slave-master. I have come to accept that Wilson, like Margaret Walker, paints a world in which the black American has had to craft a spiritual existence wholly unique and separate from what was to make living possible. And it is this process that Aunt Ester came into being to help. This process was to help her people become whole in who they are and have been. She helps them to clean their souls, to wash them, to redeem them, to find their songs and walk away singing.

Thus these plays are not at all about coming to terms with the God of *religion*. They are indeed about finding that place of redemption—of wholeness—of reconstitution. To August Wilson, the most important lesson in this cycle is **to remember—to reclaim the past**. Whether it is about seeking identity as expressed in finding your song or finding your god, the first step is **to remember**. It is the first *signpost* on the journey.

The pilgrimage begins. It walks about in the Wilson world, to live in and among his characters and his culture, to explore the redeemers, the redeemed, and the redeemable. He created them to be knowledgeable and empowered and strengthened by their past, for only by, through, and because of that past do they know who they really are. And once such knowledge is sure and sound, and the singing is full-throated, can they be free—truly a redeemed people in Canaan Land, as God intends. It is far from a God as we worship in traditional Christianity—it is not defined by

26. Margaret Walker, "We Have Been Believers." From *This Is My Century: New and Collected Poems*. Athens: University of Georgia Press, 1989. Used by permission.

doctrine—although Aunt Ester speaks at times without restraint of that God in *Gem of the Ocean*. And Stool Pigeon stitches together his own Christian theology in *King Hedley II* that works for him—and for us. *Ma Rainey's* Levee curses that God. Herald Loomis in *Joe Turner* must reject that God to find self and become free. The journeys to redemption are varied, textured, and rich. I invite you to love these plays as I place my prism before you, to love their complexity, their humor, their pathos, their sumptuous eccentricities, their faults, and their sublime beauty. Above all, love them as surely God loved the gifted man who gave them eternal life.

Arena Stage 2007 Production of *Gem of the Ocean*, with Jimonn Cole,
Lynn Godfrey, and Pascale Armand. Photo by Scott Suchman.

CHAPTER I

Gem of the Ocean

Aunt Ester

and

1839 Wylie Avenue

IT IS 1904 PITTSBURGH in the first decades of the Great Migration,[1] and *Gem of the Ocean* sets us on our maiden voyage to seek the power of redemption through history.[2] Although is it chronologically the first play, it is next to the last play Wilson wrote and had produced for performance.[3] Thus, the play's significance presents some analytical challenges, far from insurmountable, that are more importantly wonderful opportunities for deeper insight into the Cycle's most intriguing character and its sanctuary—its peaceful place.

At the time the play opens **Aunt Ester** is 285 years old. Once a slave, she is as old as the years that blacks have been on American soil.[4] She is the repository of the entire experience of blacks in America. She embodies the culture, the wisdom, the myths, the lore, the triumphs, joys, pain, suffering, hope, and the promise of her people. It is this repository that all of the

---

1. For a thorough and captivating study of the movement of African Americans from the rural south to the north during the decades of the twentieth century, see the award-winning *The Warmth of Other Suns* by Isabel Wilkerson.

2. August Wilson, *Gem of the Ocean,* set in 1904

3. It was not easy to decide whether to conduct this analysis in the order the plays were written or in the order of their chronology. The chronology wins out because of the playwright's decision to structure them in this particular way. I hope you will agree.

4. When she dies in *King Hedley II* in 1985, she is 366 years old.

1

Wilson world can tap into. August Wilson bestowed upon her the greatest importance of all of his characters.[5]

Gem is the first, and only, time in the Cycle in which she makes an actual appearance. Wilson first spoke of her publicly in 1989 when she was clearly in development. He was working on *Two Trains Running*, and described it as a 400 year-old autobiography. "I'm as old as the black experience in America. That's a deep whale. The play is about a woman named Aunt Ester . . . She's a repository of the entire experience."[6] She was designed to be him, although the play itself evolved into stories about choices—options for finding redemption. It nonetheless becomes the first time in the Cycle that Aunt Ester is mentioned and becomes a source of wisdom.

His artistic vision of Aunt Ester evolved, as well. In an enlightening and wide-ranging 1990 exchange with Wilson scholar Vera Sheppard—the date of the conversation must have been just about the time that *Two Trains* opened for performances (March 1990)[7]—Wilson acknowledges the offstage presence of 322 year-old Aunt Ester. Vera Sheppard quips that it's a good thing that she's offstage and doesn't have to be shown at that age. Wilson's response is that the makeup person would have to do a tremendous job. What comes next is the key to Aunt Ester. He says:

> But your experience is alive, your legacy is alive. All you have to do is tap into it. So at various points the characters in the play . . . go to see Aunt Ester in order to solve their problems. And she tells them a very simple thing, and that is: If you drop the ball, there is no need to run to the end zone, because there is not going to be a touchdown. You have to go back and pick up the ball.[8]

Thus it was Aunt Ester who advised her people to go back, to reclaim the past ("go back and pick up the ball"), get to the source of that which empowers and take it and move forward. Go back to the past, do not let it defeat you, but *use it* and move forward. It is that spirit which infuses all of Wilson's Cycle even though Aunt Ester is not always present to preside over it.

The estimable Phylicia Rashad gave life to *Gem's* Aunt Ester. She says that when she first spoke to August Wilson about taking on the role of

5. Wilson, "Aunt Ester's Children: A Century on Stage."

6. Watlington. "Hurdling Fences."

7. It had a long production history on its way to New York. It opened at the Yale Rep in March of 1990, but did not have its Broadway opening until April 1992.

8. Sheppard, "August Wilson: An Interview," 116–17.

Aunt Ester Tyler, he spoke of having had Aunt Ester spoken *of or about* in *Two Trains* and in *King Hedley II*. He said that he had heard his characters in those plays speak of her. Then one day while sitting in a restaurant in Pittsburgh's Hill District he heard her voice, and he wrote what she said to him on napkins, then he called his cellphone and recorded what she said. And for fear that it might be erased he called his home phone and recorded what she said to him. That was the beginning of *Gem of the Ocean*, the mother of the plays—complex poetically and rich in metaphor.[9] It is here that she leads a troubled young man through a dark and fearsome journey, and helps him back home—redeemed and whole and free.

Finally she takes on shape and form, and with the force of poetry and metaphor she dispenses her wisdom for generations of black people, slave and free, those seeking and those at home, those whose songs are still stuck in their throats and those who are singing loud and strong and clear. What she knows she will tell, and it is no great secret: that to find wholeness and serenity, to get redeemed, is an act of self. No one else can do it for you. You, and you alone must carry that ball across the goal line, as August Wilson has said of her. And as she says in *Gem* to Citizen Barlow, she cannot wash his soul clean, only he can take the steps to ask God to wash his soul. He, and he alone, must take that soul-washing journey. Or later in *Radio Golf*, Sterling reports that when he went to her because he carried around resentments because he is an orphan, she sternly told him to set it down; if he needed to pick something up, to pick up a bag of tools. Then he would have something.

She is a taskmaster. She fusses at Black Mary constantly—about the cooking, the vegetable preparation, the fire level, the manner in which guests are greeted, the way Black Mary does the laundry—until one day Black Mary explodes and becomes angry, declares her independence, that she will do everything her own way. Aunt Ester's response is quite simple. "What took you so long?"[10] Aunt Ester loves her people. She wants them to be free through remembrance and recognition of all that has happened before. Redeemed—fully redeemed—through memory, and free enough to fight back in the face of oppression.

1839 Wylie Avenue. "This a peaceful house."[11] And with those words August Wilson not only begins the Century Cycle, he establishes the pre-

---

9. See Rashad, "Foreword."

10. Wilson, *Gem,* 77.

11 Ibid., 7.

eminence of this house as the sanctuary. It is where the Cycle begins, and it is where it will end. It is a sanctuary—not a shelter. A shelter is a place of protection from the elements—from the storms. A sanctuary, however, is where you go for sustenance—for strength. People arrive, and when they do, they are offered a biscuit (bread), or beans, or greens. There is always something to eat—something to nourish and to comfort the visitor. 1839 Wylie is where Aunt Ester lives. She is the owner and its principal occupant.

It is the home where people come to encounter God, to wash their souls, to face the painful past, to try to become free, to remember, and thus to be redeemed. Eli, with the doorkeeper's opening proclamation, "This a peaceful house," sets the stage for the great transformations and journeys of spirit that are to take place, not only in this house, not only in this play, but in each person who experiences this monumental universe that comprises the Century Cycle. Of 1839 Wylie, itself a metaphor, Wilson's Black Mary says:

> A place of refuge shall be given unto you and whosoever seeketh counsel therein shall be made also clean, for I have given unto the master of that abode a place above the law, for the law is a punisher of men, and I seeketh their redemption.[12]

And thus August Wilson establishes the spiritual center of his world— a place the law will not—cannot—diminish, as it has beyond its walls for 322 years. When the fundamental values of the community are destroyed by the violence of the 1980s and people are unmindful of their past and disrespect their history, is when Aunt Ester dies with her hand stuck to head and the path to 1839 Wylie Avenue is overgrown with weeds. There is all-out mayhem in the streets of the Hill district. Aunt Ester dies of grief. Yet she is resurrected in spirit at the end, and that spirit lives on to enlighten her people.[13] Her spirit survives even when 1839 Wylie is threatened with destruction at the end of the Cycle. The sanctuary survives in spirit. Her spirit survives to dispense the wisdom to save it—that repository of memory, customs, history, and values.[14]

As Aunt Ester's home, 1839 Wylie Avenue is the Cycle's heart and soul—the refuge for weary and needy people, a Canaan, a Promised Land where a people's perambulations in and about the wilderness will stop for a

---

12. Ibid., 82.
13. Wilson, *King Hedley II*.
14. Wilson, *Radio Golf.*

rest or come to an end. They can walk away with vision and insight anew—standing upon a new tableland.

The Characters. Eli is Aunt Ester's gatekeeper, yet he never keeps anyone from entering at the appropriate time. That would not be right. The people need Aunt Ester. They may come in, but Aunt Ester can only see them on Tuesdays. Eli can only turn Citizen Barlow away when he tries to see Aunt Ester on Saturday. That is his job. But Eli is a good man—a solid man. He and Solly worked together during slavery on the Underground Railroad. Citizen Barlow is a young man—new up from the South, Alabama—in spiritual turmoil. He works at the local mill—now in complete upheaval because a falsely accused black man is dead; dead because he refused to confess to stealing a bucket of nails. The truth is that Citizen stole the nails and is wracked with so much guilt over this man's death that he can hardly wait until Tuesday to see Aunt Ester. He's heard that she will wash his soul, and that cleansing will remove the stain of guilt. But when in desperation he knocks on Saturday, Aunt Ester sees him, and notes that he reminds him of her dead son, June Bug. This is Wilson's device for the bonding that takes place between Citizen and Aunt Ester, and why she sees to it that he enters before Tuesday, and not through the front door, but by leaving a window open. Eli does not have to break his tradition, or his rule, or his allegiance to Aunt Ester.

Black Mary is a young woman and Aunt Ester's spiritual protégé and housekeeper. She has verve. We see her develop her sense of independence and freedom, and eventually the confidence that will allow her to find comfort in the arms of a newly redeemed Citizen Barlow. Rutherford Selig is a peddler who travels and is a frequent visitor to the house. Selig is often, if not always, cast as a white man, although the play's casting directions do not call for it. That racial dynamic makes sense, for Selig needs to be able to move about in places where the presence of a black man would raise suspicions. For example, toward the end of the play, Selig needs to be able to cross the river with Solly in hiding, and it would be unlikely that a black man could get of out town at that point without being subject to a thorough search.

Solly "Two Kings", born into slavery, is perhaps a suitor to Aunt Ester—there are hints of flirting (she calls him an "old rascal"). Solly is 67 years old, a wise man, and eccentric.[15] He is a familiar Wilson character-type, an

---

15. His chosen occupation is to collect pure dog shit. People, including Aunt Ester, covet it. Wilson's lesson here is that the old way is to find value—precious value—in that

odd man who in many ways exists in his own reality, yet who dispenses great wisdom—oracular wisdom. And like almost all of Wilson's oracles, Solly's brilliance is hidden beneath a thick layer of apparent madness. He is insightful, colorful, and eloquent as he instructs on what it means to be in shackles and what it means to be free. Every single one of his speeches is written to shine light and to proclaim truth. He is not only a redeemer of people, having worked tirelessly on the Underground Railroad, but he is also perhaps Wilson's most fluent, and even elegant, spokesman in the Cycle for self-determination and the complexity of freedom's value. Lastly, Solly is hilarious. To wit:

> **Solly:** My name is Two Kings. Used to be Uncle Alfred. The government looking for me for being a runaway so I changed it.

> **Citizen:** My mama named me Citizen after freedom came. She wouldn't like it if I changed my name.

> **Solly:** Your mama's trying to tell you something. She put a heavy load on you. It's hard to be a citizen. You gonna have to fight to get that. And time you get it you be surprised how heavy it is. I used to be called Uncle Alfred back in slavery. I ran into one fellow called me Uncle Alfred. I told him say, "Uncle Alfred dead." He say, "I'm looking at you." I told him, "You looking at Two Kings. That's David and Solomon." He must have had something in his ear 'cause all he heard is Solomon. He say, "I'm gonna call you Solly." The people been calling me Solly ever since. But my name is Two Kings. Some people call me Solomon and some people call me David. I answer to either one. I don't know which one God gonna call me. If he call me Uncle Alfred then we got a big fight.[16]

Caesar Wilks, 52, Black Mary's brother is the local constable who is quite pleased to have evolved to enforce the laws of the white establishment designed to contain the freed blacks who have found their way north. He is Wilson's metaphor for the white system of justice. Caesar had been a ne'er-do-well—a roustabout, selling goods and food on sidewalks, bilking poor people out of their money. Now, after a stint in jail, he in turn rents property to poor people, and when they fall behind in their rent, he evicts them, and when they have no place to go he arrests them for vagrancy. His low point

---

which most of the world would absolutely discard.

16. *Gem*, 27–28.

in *Gem* is his arrest of Aunt Ester for harboring Solly as a fugitive from justice. He murders Solly for torching the local Mill, but that frees Citizen.

There are deep reservoirs of redemption and self-determination in this play that will be repeated motifs in future parts of the Cycle. Black Mary clarifies for Citizen Barlow that, "You got to help yourself. Aunt Ester can help you if you willing to help yourself."[17] When Black Mary pens a letter for Solly to his sister, who needs him to free her from the post-freedom chain of slavery, he says to his sister, "The best faith is in yourself, even though God do have a hand in it."[18] And before Mr. Citizen goes to the City of Bones to get his soul washed, Aunt Ester makes it clear, "I can take you to that city, but you got to want to go."[19]

God decided to redeem the Israelites, had heard their moaning,[20] and appeared to Moses and sent him to free his people from Egypt.[21] And God *empowered* Moses to free His people.[22] They were not simply made free, for in the process of redemption they had to get up and go, to move, to get out of Egypt, to march, to leave, to make the motions of self-determination. "Now the Israelites went . . . out of the land of Egypt."[23] Freedom, redemption, come with a price. You want to have it enough to get up and go. The inhabitants of August Wilson's world all know, or come to know, that the price of redemption is to act.

Before Citizen Barlow is redeemed through his journey to the City of Bones, he will come to know it as a place of memory and death and resurrection. His new friends of Aunt Ester's world spin webs of enchantment of soulful tales of redemption and self-determination. He is learning that freedom is complex, and that it has its limits and responsibilities. The play becomes the narrative of his movement to freedom onto a guiltless plateau where he will take up the staff of duty.

Solly's sister is having "a hard time with freedom . . . the white peoples is gone crazy and won't let anybody leave."[24] Citizen has stolen a bucket of

---

17. Ibid., 42.

18. Ibid., 26.

19. Ibid., 56.

20. Exodus 2:24 (JPS).

21. Ibid., 3:10.

22. Ibid., 4.

23. Ibid., 13:18.

24. *Gem*, 15. See also, Wilkerson, *Warmth of Other Suns* (note 27), "Part Two: Beginnings," 19–179. White southerners resorted to taking extraordinary measures—even

nails from the mill because his boss won't pay him, and a free man should be paid for his work. His problem now is that Garret Brown was accused of being the thief and drowned in the water rather than live a lie as a wronged man. Citizen also remembers that to get out of Alabama as a free man was tough, because "they had all the roads closed to colored people."[25] For Citizen and for Solly's sister, freedom is a fine notion, but it means that you have to work to sustain it. Eli enlists Citizen to lift large stones acquired from Selig to build a fence around Aunt Ester's house in an effort to keep out those who, like Caesar, would encroach upon that freedom. They would learn that their backbreaking labor to build that fence was all for naught, for not even that fence of stone could keep their freedom inviolate from the Caesars of the world—with all of their power, despite their limitations and restrictions, they would enter with full force and with claim of right and authority.

Solly rightly warns: "You got to fight to make [freedom] mean something . . . I seen many a man die for freedom but he didn't know what he was getting. If he had known he might have thought twice about it."[26] Caesar, the evolved apologist for white oppression, has his own thwarted view of freedom from slavery and bondage. He says: "Some of these niggers was better off in slavery. They don't know how to act otherwise."[27]

Uneasy is the free Solly. He knows the duty it requires. At his first taste and smell of freedom's air, something was amiss. He couldn't enjoy it. It was Canada in 1857, and he had crossed over via the Underground Railroad. Solly just sat down and cried. He cried because of "his mama and all the others still in bondage."[28] He stopped crying and he and Eli joined the Underground Railroad. His freedom meant nothing without paying the price, the duty, of redeeming others. He took sixty-two across the border until

---

terror—to making deals with Railroads to keep them from stopping at certain towns, snatching tickets from the hands of black migrants, etc., to keep blacks in the South. Whites were determined to keep the poorly compensated labor.

25. *Gem*, 22.

26. Ibid., 29. There is a clear echo of the newly freed Israelites grumbling to Moses and Aaron in the desert: "If only we had died by the hand of the Lord in the land of Egypt, when we sat by the fleshpots, when we ate our fill of bread! For you have brought us out into this wilderness to starve this whole congregation to death" (Exodus 16:3; JPS).

27. *Gem*, 36. It distresses me that both Solly and Caesar arrive at the same point— Solly enlightened and Caesar's lamp quite dim; that freedom is illusive and far from being a wholly joyous state.

28. Ibid., 59.

January 1, 1863,[29] when Lincoln freed the slaves. Citizen Barlow would take up the new cause of redemption after Solly's death.

The children of Israel came to know full well the cost of being a freed people. With great and justifiable expectation, the Hebrews in bondage—like Solly on his journey to Canada—dreamt of a kinder and even Arcadian world. The Israelites met with the reality of a harsh and unyielding desert with unforgiving elements. No Arcadia here—no peaceful house—not yet. Surely it was deflating after the exhilarating defeat of Pharaoh's army at the Red Sea.[30] Anticipation and expectation, and perhaps even fantasy, met with the harsh glare of truth. With liberation comes responsibility—perhaps even poignant regret.

Aunt Ester, Solly, Eli, and Black Mary instruct Citizen that the cost of freedom is to help yourself. God can part the Sea, but you have to walk through. God can make the water sweet and potable, but you have to drink it and obey Him.[31] The will to be redeemed must be strong. The determination to walk, to drink, to do, to obey, to travel, to remember, to pick up and to set down heavy stones—must be unshakable; and the desire to have your soul washed is the theme of *Gem of the Ocean*.

Memory: the power of memory. August Wilson wants his people to know who we are. And to know who we are we need to know from whence we have come. Remember. Aunt Ester tells us:

> I got a strong memory. I got a long memory. People say you crazy to remember. But I ain't afraid to remember. I try to remember out loud. I keep my memories alive. I feed them. I got to feed them otherwise they'd eat me up. I got memories go way back. I'm carrying them for a lot of folk. All the old-timey folks. I'm carrying their memories, and I'm carrying my own.[32]

She says this poem, sings this song, really, this sublime ode to her special place in this epic cycle of work—the repository of it all—all that is African in American culture, and from the beginning. It is a hymn of praise to the

29. At 12:01 am, January 1, 1863, President Abraham Lincoln's Emancipation Proclamation took effect.

30. Exodus 14:30 (JPS).

31. Ibid., 15:24–26. After the Israelites decamped, there was no potable water. God made the water sweet and promised not to visit upon them the plagues he set upon the Egyptians, in exchange for the Israelites' obedience.

32. *Gem*, 45.

power of knowing, and the free air and fuel for the job of a free people that can come from knowing. Could it be any lovelier?

The late Rev. Professor Peter Gomes, who from 1974 until his death in 2010 served as the Pusey Minister in Harvard's Memorial Church and as Harvard's Plummer Professor of Christian Morals, understood the power of memory and its intrinsic link to freedom. He preached one Pentecost Sunday on "Remembrance and Imagination." Ever inventive and intellectually deft, he said, "Acts of remembrance are keys to imagination . . . If you remember you can imagine."[33] Without taking issue with this assumption, for it is true enough to be acceptable for these purposes, he continues:

> it is the use of the imagination that sets the spirit free. It is the use of the imagination that allows the Holy Spirit . . . to be set free in each and every one of us, giving us the appearance at times of being drunk and out of control and without a plan, and yet it is that very spirit-filled imagination that sets us free.[34]

Gomes preaches the power of redemption through memory that releases the soul to soar, to move, to get up, to step up, to wander.

God directs remembrance of the time he redeems Israel. "This day shall be to you one of remembrance . . . you shall celebrate it as an institution *for all time*."[35] **For all time**. Do not forget that you are a freed people, and I did it. For all time. August Wilson understood the necessity of memory and was frustrated not only by white destruction and erasure of Black America's history but by its own apparent loss of its sense of history and its gravity. He recalled having gone to a Seder at Passover and could not fathom why Black America does not celebrate the Emancipation Proclamation in a similar way, for "it would give us a way of identifying and expressing our unity."[36]

Wilson addresses these questions of memory and redemption when he brings Citizen and Aunt Ester together to connect Citizen with the ancestors. Citizen arrives at 1839 Wylie Avenue as a fugitive from memory, and leaves a full member of the community—able to face the ugly truths of his past—his soul frightfully yet lovingly cleansed to receive the pathos and its ecstasy, triumphs and defeat, dishonors and glories—all of it.

With all that power of the past, Aunt Ester prepares to take Mr. Citizen to the City of Bones. It is that mythical place in the center of the Atlantic

---

33. Gomes, *Strength for the Journey*, 294.

34. Ibid., 295.

35. Exodus 12:14 (JPS); emphasis added.

36. Lyons, "Interview with August Wilson: 1997," 210.

Ocean where the ship, the Gem of the Ocean, sank with the bodies of Africans chained together and bound for slavery in America. It is as far back as our memories can take us to our American or African pasts. It is as far back as we can go to connect us to our ancestors—a mid-ocean floor. It is reminiscent of the Amiri Baraka poem:

> It's my brother, my sister.
> At the bottom of the Atlantic Ocean there's a
> Railroad made of human bones
>> Black ivory
>> Black ivory[37]

It is also, of course, a likely metaphor for the valley of dry bones in the vision written by or about the prophet Ezekiel, who prophesies as the Lord directs, and the bones take on sinew and flesh and are lifted up from their graves and brought to the land of Israel.[38] Resurrected, redeemed, free. Mr. Citizen takes this mythic voyage, assisted by Aunt Ester, Black Mary, Solly, and Eli. It is beautiful and terrifying. Yet they reassure him as he approaches the Twelve Gates of the City.[39] It is a restored city of Jerusalem, an Eden, a place of refuge—Aunt Ester's house, to which Mr. Citizen needs entry in order to be redeemed. The gatekeeper this time, however, is not Eli who readily admits him. It is Garret Brown, the man who stood falsely accused of stealing the bucket of nails from the mill that Citizen actually stole. Mr. Brown bars Citizen's entry to the City of Bones. Wilson references the prohibition from Revelation that no one enters the city who "practices . . . falsehood . . ."[40] Citizen, counseled by Aunt Ester to cleanse his soul by telling the truth, admits the theft, and Brown admits Citizen to see the Beautiful City with people who have tongues on fire.[41] He returns to 1839 Wylie a redeemed soul.

When Caesar shoots and kills Solly for burning the mill, Citizen Barlow sees his calling—his price of freedom—his duty. He removes from Solly's body his hat and coat, takes his stick and heads for the South to free Solly's sister and other blacks who cannot leave. The others stand and toast Solly—"So Live"—so live to see to the liberation of others. So live as Citizen Barlow has begun to do: to live into his name—citizen—to step out and onto higher ground as a redeemer of souls, and a repository of the history of his people.

37. Baraka, "Improvisation on *Wise, Why's, Y's*." Used by permission.
38. Ezekiel 37: 7–14 (JPS).
39. Nehemiah 3 (JPS).
40. Revelation 21:27 (NRSV).
41. *Gem*, 71.

Arena Stage 1987 Production of *Joe Turner's Come and Gone* with Delroy Lindo, Kippen Hay, and LaFontaine Oliver. Photo by Joan Marcus.

Chapter II

I'm Standing Now!

Herald Loomis Redeemed

Joe Turner's Come and Gone

Luminous and transfigured, Herald Loomis gloriously proclaims, "I'm standing now!" It came to August Wilson in a raging snowstorm in a Grand Avenue Bar in St. Paul, Minnesota. The hours of December 1, 1983 were waning, and the play had to be put in the mail by midnight to make the O'Neill deadline.[1] Wilson had no idea what Martha and Loomis would say to one another upon meeting after so many years apart. When he sat down that night, he did not know what was to happen. This was to be the closing scene of the play. He wrote it in twenty-five minutes, not changing a word of it, and when finished he was soaked in sweat. He said, "I was there at the house of God. I was there . . . and I had my play."[2]

It was a unique creative experience for him—to write with such sure inspiration—and it would be the capstone to *Joe Turner's Come and Gone*, his admittedly favorite play of the Cycle.[3] And from that point in the Wilson imagination, a home like that in Pittsburgh would become a sacred space—a space where lost souls could find their song and their way to that

---

1. The Eugene O'Neill Theater Center's 1984 National Playwright's Conference.

2. Lyons, "Interview," 216.

3. August Wilson, *Joe Turner's Come and Gone*, set in 1911. Wilson often spoke of *Joe Turner* as being his favorite. Query whether he continued to think so after *Gem of the Ocean* had been written and performed? He began to write *Radio Golf* almost immediately after *Gem*, and death soon followed. Both *Joe Turner* and *Gem* are epic in scope and deeply resonant in metaphor and meaning. They are rivals in the Cycle—to me.

road to redemption. The place of creation, this sacred space, this house of God, would be an Eden, and a place of beauty and serenity. A place to be nourished and to be healed. It would be a peaceful house—this mythical and mystical 1839 Wylie Avenue.

> From the deep and the near South the sons and daughters of newly freed African slaves wander into the city, isolated, cut off from memory, having forgotten the names of the gods and only guessing at their faces, they arrive dazed and stunned, their heart kicking in their chest with a song worth singing. They arrive carrying Bibles and guitars, their pockets lined with dust and fresh hope, marked men and women seeking to scrape . . . a way of . . . shaping the malleable parts of themselves into a new identity as free men of definite and sincere worth.
>
> Foreigners in a strange land, they carry as part and parcel of their baggage a long line of separation and dispersement which informs their sensibilities and marks their conduct as they search for ways to reconnect, to reassemble . . . [4]

After the complexities of coming to terms with the meaning of freedom in *Gem of the Ocean*, in *Joe Turner* Wilson wrestles with identity. How does a person, newly released from a Joe Turner's post-emancipation slavery, know who or what he is? This man, Herald Loomis, never knew actual slavery, yet was snatched from all he knew—his wife, child, his kith and kin—and from his poor sharecropping existence. In *Joe Turner* Wilson takes on slavery's destruction of heritage, family, ancestry, culture. Its main character sets out on the road in search of who he is, and who and where the mother of his child is. It is a fundamental human longing. All that anchors humanity is gone—demolished by the experience of slavery and its legacy. The descendants of slaves have to bring it all back together—overcome the fierce opposition to memory—to bring it back. *Joe Turner* does that for us, and in that reassembly is its power.

Its traveler goes back to where he came from, and they are all gone. Some are dead. Some have since just disappeared, as if they had evanesced. Most have departed to go to this place or that. Scattered. He must find them. He must find someone who can tell him. Point him the way. He must see his child, his wife. What happened to his mother, his father? Who is he, now? Wilson's literary and dramatic device is to strip him bare, such that we can

---

4 Wilson, *Joe Turner*, 6.

watch him take on the essential pieces of his identity that were sliced away from his soul when Joe Turner snatched him up and put him in shackles.

Yes. He must find his identity. He must find his song—that which makes him who he is, what makes his heart soar, ache, beat day, beat night, race fast in fear, slow down to rest, long for the spirit, and long for love—love of friends, family, and a woman. He must know—remember—the pain of the past, but he has to be free of its weighty stones of fear and pain that keep him from standing on his own two feet. Like Lazarus, he must be raised and unbound.[5] He must be cleansed, baptized, redeemed. He must come to know God again—that he is a child of God, and that this deep and profound longing is a longing for the love of God.

Herald Loomis is that man. Loomis was not born into slavery, and as a young man was a deacon in the Abundant Life Church. While on the road, he came upon a crap game, and stopped to preach to the gamblers. Suddenly he was taken by Joe Turner, and like many others, taken against his will and under slave-like conditions, held for seven years.

His daughter, Zonia, was just a nursing baby when all of this happened. Upon his release, Loomis went back to find Martha, his wife, but she had already moved away somewhere to find work. She had reportedly given up on Loomis for dead. Zonia now lived with Martha's mother, and Herald took her on the road with him to find her mother and his wife. That brought him with Zonia in hand to the sanctuary that was Seth and Bertha Holly's house in Pittsburgh in 1911. It is there that his longing ends, he finds himself, his song, "which is both a wail and whelp of joy,"[6] and yet one more of Aunt Ester's children, lit from within, is redeemed.

August Wilson spoke forthrightly about the inspiration for *Joe Turner*. He said that from Romare Bearden he learned that "the fullness and richness of everyday ritual life can be rendered without compromise or sentimentality."[7] *Joe Turner* is true to its inspiration. Wilson paints an unsparing portrait of the people who come in and out of the Holly sanctuary. It is practically axiomatic that *Joe Turner* came about after Wilson beheld Bearden's "Mill Hand's Lunch Bucket," a collage and watercolor of a boarding house in 1920s Pittsburgh. A man sits at a table in apparent defeat. It captured Wilson's imagination. "That man became Herald Loomis."[8]

---

5. John 11:43–44 (NRSV).

6. *Joe Turner*, 6.

7. Plimpton, "August Wilson: The Art of Theater."

8. Powers, "An Interview with August Wilson," 7.

Seth and Bertha Holly are stable. Married for twenty-five years, they own and operate a boarding house in Pittsburgh's Hill District. They are church-going and decent people who run a respectable establishment, as Seth Holly quickly reminds everybody who stops by to inquire about a room. Bertha keeps the house and provides a kind, but firm, complement to Seth's often-brusque tone. She serves the "communion meal." Everyone who arrives, even for just a while, is offered a biscuit, that form of basic sustenance. The people are each unique with singular outlooks, visions, and hopes. However, as at the Eucharist, differences—political, moral, and theological—are set aside at Bertha's common table, and the meal is shared as one community.[9] Thus this house, not unlike Aunt Ester's 1839 Wylie Avenue, is a peaceful house—a "good house."[10] It is a place where Herald Loomis will encounter God, where he will come to know who he is.

Bynum, one of the boarders of long-standing, provides early in the play what will become in this and other plays of the Cycle the source of fundamental tension between African mysticism, religions, customs, mores, metaphysical beliefs, and Christianity. Perhaps it isn't tension, but a complex coexistence, and a necessary function of black hope, belief, and survival in white, enslaving America—a white America that wanted sole ownership of that Christian God, and probably wanted to dictate the terms of God's relationship with the enslaved Africans.

Bynum raises pigeons out back of the house, and carries on rituals with their blood, making sacrificial offerings, performing an occasional ceremonial dance—especially in the mornings. Seth complains that it's all that "heebie-jeebie" stuff, and is quite gruff about it, yet follows Bertha's wisdom and mostly leaves Bynum in peace.

Bynum is *Joe Turner's* oracle. He wants Rutherford Selig,[11] the white "people finder," to find the Shiny Man he's been looking for. As a boy, Selig

9. This is also a point at which the audience might discern (depending, of course on the director) aspects of liturgy in corporate eating rituals that anchor meals (communion) as a form of worship. There is repetition in prayer, in the intonation, and in the elevation of the "everyday" and the "ordinary" that frees the worshipper (and in turn, the audience) to enjoy a fuller appreciation and knowledge (discernment) of the divine in what is occurring. A keen ear will also (and always) hear the playwright's peerless lyrical style.

10. *Joe Turner*, 18. I think for August Wilson students it is safe and right to consider the Holly home to be an early 1839 Wylie, even though at the time the play was conceived, Aunt Ester had not yet taken form in Wilson's imagination. It is, after all, that place of refuge that 1839 Wylie becomes.

11. Rutherford Selig was the white traveling peddler from *Gem*. He returns here, still peddling—of sorts.

helped his father and grandfather find escaped slaves, and returned them to their owners. When freedom came, he became a people finder to help "nigras" who became scattered to find one another. Bertha is not so sure. She thinks, "He ain't never found nobody he ain't took away."[12] And because Seth peddles pots and pans door-to-door, he sees where people are living. That makes it easy to find out who is where. He peddles cheap kitchenware goods, and he peddles empty hope. It's all the same to him, I suppose.

Bynum described for Selig the Shiny Man, who Bynum saw on the road. The Shiny Man rubbed his hands in blood in a ritual cleansing, and then disappeared. Bynum then saw his ancestor, his dead father, who taught Bynum how to find his song—his identity—and then said to Bynum that if he ever saw a Shiny Man again he would know that his song had been accepted, and he could die a happy man. His song was the Binding Song. That is why Bynum sticks people together. That is why he is called Bynum—"Bind Them." "Just like glue I sticks people together."[13] He does just that, just as he bridges worlds of African religion, mysticism, culture, and Christianity. Bynum has charged Selig with finding the "Shiny Man."

Joe Turner is a tableau of human longing—for identity, for love, for a voice, for God; that wholeness, a place of redemption. Everyone who comes into the house to stay is a seeker—a descendant of a slave's journey. The greatest of the all the seekers is Herald Loomis—a hulking presence with a decidedly menacing look that barely masks a core of memory and suffering. What unsettles Seth Holly is what he sees as Loomis's unmistakably incipient rage—perhaps even a touch of explosive lunacy. His stare is searching and piercing. But what softens him and makes him less terrifying is the warmth with which he regards his daughter, Zonia, who accompanies him and clearly adores him, trusts him, and he holds lovingly by her hand. He searches for her mother (and his wife), Martha. Wilson says of him, "He is at times possessed. A man driven not so much by hellhounds that seemingly bay at his heels, but by his *search for a world that speaks to something about himself* . . . he seeks to re-create the world into one that *contains his image*."[14] He needs to be in a place where he is not some alien, where there are people who look, act, and feel like him. He must be redeemed. He searches for the will and the ability to stand on his own. He employs Selig

12. *Joe Turner*, 42.

13. Ibid., 16.

14. Ibid., 18–19; emphasis added.

to help him find Martha Loomis, but finding her will not be sufficient; it will take more. Bynum has the key.

Loomis is unaware that Seth, Bertha, and Bynum all know that Martha is in town, and that she has actually been in the Holly boarding house to see Bynum. She came to ask Bynum to find her daughter, Zonia. They also know, but do not disclose, that she is now an evangelical Christian, and has changed her name to Martha Pentecost, to reflect her fundamentalist evolution, and the specific reference to the future mention of the Holy Ghost.[15] Fearing for Martha's safety, Seth and Bertha resist disclosing this information to Loomis.

The Great Redemption Rituals. Wilson presents the great redemption rituals for Loomis in two stages—each one a profound celebration of African culture and its subsisting tension with American religious and cultural values. They are not conflicting for those assembled in the sanctuary except one—there is an acceptable coexistence as it will be with Aunt Ester. The tension is with Herald Loomis. The tension is *within* Herald Loomis. As a metaphor for the African in America, after two dramatic encounters, it is resolved, it seems. But how?

The first ritual begins just after the assembled boarders have enjoyed an old-fashioned, after-church, Sunday evening fried-chicken supper. At Seth's urging they decide to Juba, apparently a Sunday tradition of the Holly household. A Juba is a dance, similar to the call-and-response dances of the African slaves. Wilson's stage directions (rarely appearing in the text of the play, as they do here) are firm and clear. "It should be as African as possible, with the performers working themselves up into a near frenzy. The words can be improvised, but should include some mention of the Holy Ghost."[16] The conflict is set—the God of the enslaved versus the God of the enslaver.

As the Juba reaches a near frenzy, enters Herald Loomis who seizes upon the mention of the Holy Ghost, recalls his capture by Joe Turner, becomes furious and incoherent, screaming about the silliness of tongues of fire burning up woolly heads (for Loomis, a Christian God would only destroy black people) and then he, himself, starts speaking in tongues while dancing around the kitchen, then collapses onto the floor. He embodies the African-American internal strife in worshipping a God who also loves and redeems the enslaver. It appears as if it will destroy him if left unresolved.

---

15. The Christian Pentecost is based on the New Testament (Acts 2:1–31) when the Holy Spirit descended upon the Apostles as tongues of fire.

16. *Joe Turner*, 50.

Loomis was seized by Joe Turner while preaching Christian doctrine. He has little use for it now. He wants nothing of this Christianity. It sets him off. He sees visions now, and he reacts to what he alone sees.

Seth, Bertha, and the others are all alarmed and frightened, but not Bynum, the one person who understands this longing for identity and redemption. He calmly and with confidence engages Loomis on what Loomis sees. Loomis speaks of bones rising up out of the water, and how they rise on top of it, marching in a line (prompts Bynum), and then they all sink down creating a wave that washes them ashore as black people with flesh and bones. Loomis is among them. They get up and walk toward a road, but Loomis cannot. They scatter. Like the slaves sold into bondage and now free, they go in all directions, waving goodbye. Loomis cannot get up. He is still bound. He cannot stand. Not yet. No song for him. Not yet.

This metaphor for the death and resurrection of those Africans who did not make it through the Middle Passage is a theme in the Cycle that makes its debut in *Joe Turner*.[17] The interpretation finding its basis in the book of the prophet Ezekiel has validity according to Wilson's dramaturge Todd Kreidler.[18]

Loomis's frightening display of apparent lunacy confirms Seth Holly's worst fears about him, and he makes clear to Loomis and everyone in the house that he wants Loomis gone—out of the house by week's end. In fact, Loomis is given a day certain to be cleared out. It further reinforces Seth's decision that he and Bertha were right in not telling Loomis the exact whereabouts of Martha Loomis Pentecost. Convinced that Loomis is not right in the head, Seth fears that Loomis might harm Martha. But Loomis has calmed down. He has begun to be attracted to another boarder, Mattie

17. There are resonances in *Gem*, when Citizen makes his journey to the City of Bones. One could argue, of course, that the redemption he finds there is a resurrection—a new life—born again in the Christian sense. Such an interpretation is intriguing (if not beguiling) for our purposes. I would doubt that Wilson would find that interpretation compelling, as he does not appear to be especially moved by Christian doctrine. Additionally, debut is an apt term, for *Joe Turner* was written several years prior to *Gem*, and any Middle Passage references are in fact "firsts."

18. Conversation with Todd Kreidler, Pasadena, CA, October 18, 2012. Although Kreidler was not a part of the Wilson creative team at the time when *Joe Turner* was written, he was writing with Wilson when the bones re-entered the Cycle in *Gem*. He was regaled with long stories of the loud and sometimes hysterical theological arguments between Wilson and Rev. Dwight Andrews about the meaning of Ezekiel's bones gaining sinew, flesh, and breath. (Ezekiel 37:8–9). Rev. Andrews served as the musical director for *Joe Turner* at Yale, Arena Stage, and for the Broadway run. He is now a minister serving in Atlanta, GA.

Campbell, and she to him. In one poignant scene he moves closer, expressing how much woman he sees in her, and as he searches for the words and gestures of desire he says instead, with sadness and regret, "I done forgot how to touch."[19]

Shortly before Loomis's eviction day, Bynum sits around the house seemingly busy in idle things and sings old camp songs, including one about "Joe Turner's come and gone." This, of course, goads Loomis into talking about his seven years of feeling worthless under Turner.[20] The poetry here, however, belongs to Bynum, who tells Loomis that all will be well when he finds his song. He says to Loomis, "What [Joe Turner] wanted was your song. He wanted to have that song to be his. He thought that by catching you he could learn that song . . . But you still got it. You just forgot how to sing it."[21]

When your identity is gone, your freedom is gone. How can you be free if you don't know who you are? How can you sing your song of freedom if you can't find it? Singing the song has always been the triumphant way to celebrate freedom. The moment the Israelites knew that Pharaoh's army had been vanquished and that they were free, they sang, "I will sing to the Lord, for he has triumphed gloriously."[22] Miriam sang the song to proclaim the new freedom.[23] Something would have to shatter, break, explode, shred to get Loomis to find that song.

And, behold, the veil of the temple was rent
in twain from the top to the bottom[24]

Loomis is gone and standing with Zonia on a nearby corner. Bertha engages in a ritual dance—a cleansing—that chases away the sadness. It is "her own remedy that is centuries old and to which she is connected by the muscles of her heart and the blood's memory."[25] It is meant to convey

---

19. *Joe Turner*, 73.

20. The worthlessness of black men is a theme that appears in later plays in the Cycle, most notably in *Seven Guitars*, as Floyd "Schoolboy" Barton is thrown in jail because the Judge prior to sentencing him for vagrancy off-handedly said, "You're just worthless." Floyd says from that point on that he served time in jail for being "worthless."

21. *Joe Turner*, 70.

22. Exodus 15:1 (JPS).

23. Ibid., 15:21.

24. Matthew 27:51 (KJV).

25. *Joe Turner*, 79–80. This is reminiscent of Yoruban customs of dancing to chase away evil spirits and to restore peace—a ritual cleansing. This ancient West African

joy and restore peace and harmony. Yet it is not the kind of harmony that Bertha anticipates. She believes that the house is now free of Loomis's odd spirit, but Wilson has other plans. She is actually preparing the sanctuary, not in gratitude for what has just departed, but for what is to come—a baptism, a naming. It will be the play's second great ritual. And no one knows it at this time. They think that all the "heebie-jeebie" stuff is finished. Back to normal, with a little of Bynum thrown in for spice. But Selig, the intrepid, and almost-too-successful people-finder that he is, arrives with the long-lost Martha Loomis Pentecost. Within seconds, Loomis and Zonia re-enter.

Bynum confesses to binding Martha to her daughter. Loomis misunderstands it as an effort to bind him, and sets upon Bynum with a knife. But Bynum again takes charge, and Martha provides the essential pull in the opposite direction. Bynum calmly assures Loomis that he is on the verge of being able to sing his song. Martha, on the other hand, seeing that Loomis has taken a knife, and fearing that he will attack at random, begins shouting that he must look to Jesus. She recites passages of the 23rd Psalm,[26] using the metaphor of the valley of death, and Loomis exclaims that death's valleys are where he has been, and that he has seen a grinning Jesus in the middle of niggers wallowing at his feet. He says, "Great big old white man . . . your Mr. Jesus Christ . . . talk about what a nice man Mr. Jesus Christ is 'cause he give him salvation after he die. Something wrong here. Something don't fit right!"[27] The white man's God is not for him a source of redemption. It is over for him and Martha. She is still bound. He has to move on. He knows that now. Christianity is an ill-fitting garment that pinches and binds. Bynum knows this. Bynum understands this. Bynum now has to deliver Loomis.

Martha continues to proclaim the need to have faith in Jesus, and that Jesus offers salvation. Loomis screams that his enemies are all around "picking flesh from my bones. I'm choking on my own blood and all you got to give me is salvation?"[28] She tells him to be washed in the blood of the lamb.

Voices are raised and the tension is as if audiences are not present at all—intensely quiet. Loomis screams out as he takes the knife and slashes

---

custom is carried out with apparent ease by this devout Christian woman—two religious traditions and cultures in peaceful and comfortable coexistence.

26. "Yea, though I walk through the valley of the shadow of death, I will fear no evil . . . " Psalm 23:4 (KJV).

27. Ibid., 85.

28. Ibid.

himself across his chest. Twice. Drawing blood. Rubbing it across his face. "I don't need nobody to bleed for me! I can bleed for myself."

He is cleansed, washed in his own blood, baptized, named, given breath, redeemed, raised, born again, lifted, freed, identified. He is self-sufficient and resurrected. Those bones now with black flesh have not left him behind, and he exclaims as a free man, a full soul: "I'm standing! I'm standing. My legs stood up! I'm standing now!"

And finally Bynum tells him, "Herald Loomis, you shining! You shining like new money!" Transfigured. Lit. Lit from within.

Arena Stage 2002 Production of *Ma Rainey's Black Bottom*,
with Tina Fabrique. Photo by Scott Suchman.

CHAPTER III

God Hate Niggers

The Tragedy

of

Ma Rainey's Black Bottom

"GOD HATE NIGGERS."[1] JUST one. Just one of several verbal assaults the audience has to endure before packing up to leave the world of *Ma Rainey's Black Bottom*. Brilliantly crafted—each character in the band speaking in the cadence associated with his name (Slow Drag, Cutler, or a Toledo)—*Ma Rainey* has gorgeous soliloquies, each one infused with the rhythm and pathos of the blues. They are blues arias, actually, a theatrical art form that will see more life as we move further into the Cycle. *Ma Rainey* is where Wilson steeps his audience into the singular importance of the blues in the life and culture of blacks in America, and how essential it is to the entire American cultural conversation. It is the song; it is the black song; it is the song the Wilson men and women must find to know who they are. The blues in the Century Cycle is the existential metaphor for identity and freedom—a redeemed soul. Absent the blues, America would be singing its song in a flatter tone, without texture, without richness, lacking the depth of truth of love or pain, or joy and grief. He asks in the harshest way imaginable in *Ma Rainey*, is this what God intends?

Ma Rainey takes place in 1927 Chicago, the only play in the Cycle that is not sited in Pittsburgh's Hill District.[2] Its primary character, whether or

1. August Wilson, *Ma Rainey's Black Bottom*, set in 1927; 80.

2. Chicago, however, serves as a place—a mecca of sorts, a place of imagination—for characters in future plays such as *Seven Guitars* in which Floyd "Schoolboy" Barton

not she is on the stage, is the great blues singer of the era, Gertrude (Ma) Rainey (1886–1939), who against all odds "crossed over" and, along with Bessie Smith, was among the first black singers to record on a white label. Ma is grand, she is domineering and bombastic, and she knows and fully understands her craft and her great gift. Although *Ma Rainey* audiences can be lulled into the cadences and the rhythms of Wilson's sublime poetry,[3] eventually the cutting pain goes deep. Whatever escape we are permitted is the escape of a possibility of hope—affirming, fortuitous, episodic happiness perhaps, and maybe even momentary joy. But such is the nature of the blues. Just as it is and can be. Such is the nature of redemption as Wilson has it here—fleeting, evanescent.

Wilson's *Ma Rainey* is all of the historic Ma Rainey—and more. She first had life at the Eugene O'Neill Center in Waterford, Connecticut, in 1982. Frank Rich, then chief drama critic for the *New York Times*, said he "half-violated" the O'Neill rule about press coverage. He watched in amazement and heard Levee's explosive speech, then wrote a column in the *Times* about the excitement of this new and unknown playwright.[4]

Wilson's Ma Rainey commands—demands—respect from the men who otherwise occupy the play.[5] The talk about her dominates the dialogue before her arrival—what she wants, whether she will arrive on time, whether she will behave long enough to record the songs, whether she will pretend to be the Mother, or the Queen, of the Blues.[6] These are the minimizing questions and concerns of the recording studio's white owners. They want to control her, overpower her—just long enough to finish the recording session. To get her voice recorded is the goal of the day, perhaps a metaphor

---

dreams of returning to Chicago to record a hit record, or that place where Ruby, in *King Hedley II* (who has made an appearance in *Seven Guitars*), has been singing with a band for several preceding years.

3. Slow Drag: [to Cutler] " . . . We been doing this together for twenty-two years. All up and down the back roads, the side roads, the front roads . . . We done played the juke joints, the whorehouses, the barn dances, and city sit downs . . . I done lied for you and lied with you . . . We done laughed together, fought together, slept in the same bed together, done sucked on the same titty . . . and now you don't wanna give me no reefer." Wilson, *Ma Rainey*, 22.

4. Rich, "Foreword," xiii.

5. The exception is her romantic interest, a young woman Dussie Mae, who is portrayed as Ma's "play thing," a refinement that Levee does not comprehend, as he makes several unsuccessful amorous moves on Dussie Mae.

6. *Ma Rainey*, 10.

for the extent—the outer limit—of their care for her (and any other black woman). Get what they need and move on. Deplete and discard.

Ma knows of her limited utility to them, and she will take her own good time and drag out the session for as long as she sees fit. It is her way of holding onto her power for as long as she pleases. White men will not force her to move faster than she wants, nor to sing what she does not want to sing, or to sing in any way that does not please her artistic sensibilities. She understands all too well that the minute the recording is done, for them, so is she.

The black musicians who comprise the band are not at all troubled or otherwise concerned about Ma's idiosyncrasies. They simply accept that Ma is in charge, not the white recording studio owners. Ma is their boss, and what she says is what is going to happen. Toledo, Slow Drag, and Cutler have been with her for some time; only Levee is new. The paradox is that Levee has cut a side deal with the white owners to play Ma's song a new way—a new "cross-over" way. The guys in the band see trouble because they know that Ma will have it her way only. Levee does not understand this—convinced that whatever the white man says goes; he fails to grasp the power of the black woman artist, the recording star, the musical heavyweight who can make it happen, or not. Levee trusts the white man, who then betrays him in front of everybody in the band and he is humiliated. Toledo, Cutler, and Slow Drag are not surprised; they have seen this before. Levee has miscalculated. The white sleight of hand made the scales fall from his eyes.

The Songs of Redemption. There is a duet in *Ma Rainey*. The first voice belongs to the title character. She has it figured out. And even though she, as a black woman, cannot completely conduct and command and control her world, she wields as much power as she conceivably can. Her journey to that place in the Chicago recording studio has preceded the opening of the play. Her fame is secure, her dues paid—several times over, the tough road to Queen of the Blues already travelled, she knows her song, she knows who she is, and she stands on a Tableland as a free black woman, whose song and gifts permit the world to push her only as far as she will permit. She is fiercely independent. She openly flaunts her girlfriend, her lesbian lover, Dussie Mae—her pretty plaything—to be pampered, toyed with, dressed up, fluffed up, fussed over, powdered, bathed, kept. Dussie Mae is objectified. She is lovely to behold, with "sensual energy which seems to flow from her."[7]

7. Ibid., 36.

The impression is that there isn't as much love between them as much as an *arrangement*. Although Dussie Mae does not succumb to Levee's sexual advances, she doesn't shy away either. She likes the attention. Ma's openness about her relationship with Dussie Mae is a function of her sense of power and greatness as an artist and as a star. Few people in the 1920s would have been able to pull it off without destroying their careers. But, then again, she sang the blues, which some people regarded as so secular as to ignore God. Actually, some religious people referred to the earliest blues songs as "devil songs."[8] Ma Rainey has worked hard and has earned the respect of all the people around her. She has thus worked out her own redemption. And she has earned the privileges of taunting and teasing the honky-tonk world by dangling her "lesbian gal" in front of everybody knowing how much they want her, too. It's yet another metaphor for control—another perk of power—of having arrived. It may even be a measure of hostility for the dimmer lights that are the men around her.

The second voice of the duet is Levee's. He is the youngest of the men in the band. He is a gifted musician and talented trumpeter, unseasoned by years, and like many a youth at the beginning of his journey, is wont to meander by following judgments of an unbaked heart. His missteps are understandable, but costly. In this Wilson drama, he has the "warrior spirit" that makes him impetuous and prone to make bad choices. His mistakes make us cringe, but at least we know how he got there and why. Like the blues he plays with a riveting depth of truth and abandonment that belies his few years, his words and deeds emanate from some great internal gash of suffering. Levee's longing in *Ma Rainey* is for his own song—it is his search for his God, rejecting the God he knew, and in the process Levee takes a life.

Ma's exercise of power can be quixotic. Her entrance is complicated by a police officer who accuses her of assault and battery for having hit a cab driver with her car door. The officer does not believe it is her car (too fancy for a colored woman), and he wants to run her into the station along with her nephew and Dussie Mae for creating a disturbance. White Mr. Irving straightens it out with the cop.[9] Ma is livid and perhaps humiliated, but what shows is her anger. It is all revealed in her star-turn, erratic behavior. It is Wilson's device to demonstrate that Ma Rainey *must* exercise power—over her life, over her art, over her being, over her identity. Her

8. Cone, *Spirituals and the Blues*, 98–99.
9. *Ma Rainey*, 40.

blackness precludes such full exercise of power, but she has the gift of the blues, a voice with which to sing it, and like Herald Loomis of *Joe Turner*, it is her song and she will sing it when and how she is good and ready. It is *her* freedom song, *her* redemption.

When Irving tries to convince her to sing the song Levee's way, she responds, "I'm singing *Ma Rainey's* song. I ain't singing Levee's song. Now that's all there is to it . . . Ma listens to *her* heart. Ma listens to the voice inside *her*. That's what counts with Ma."[10] She knows her song.

She then teaches what she believes the nature of the blues to be, and the importance of the blues to black people. The play, itself, much like the tension between African spirituality and the Christian God in *Joe Turner*[11] and throughout the Cycle, sets up this constant tension between the black and white search for the inner sense of freedom and serenity. In the blues, Wilson senses an immediate emotional response rooted in his blackness— a sudden awareness that the blues spoke to his blackness and it possessed him and he it.[12] He has Ma Rainey go on eloquently about the blues:

> White folks don't understand the blues. They hear it come out but they don't know how it got there. They don't understand that's life's way of talking. You don't sing to feel better. You sing 'cause that's a way of understanding life . . . . The blues help you get out of bed in the morning. You get up knowing you ain't alone. There's something else in the world. Something's been added by that song. This be an empty world without the blues. I take that emptiness and try to fill it up with something . . . . I ain't started the blues way of singing. The blues always been here.[13]

This is Wilson's ode to the centrality of the blues—not only in *Ma Rainey*, but also in the Cycle and in his life. It began when he first heard Bessie Smith sing "Nobody in Town Can Bake a Sweet Jelly Roll Like Mine," and he practically wore it out he played it so many times. He had found his muse. And the blues would saturate all of his work from that point on. To wit: "You get up knowing you ain't alone. There's something else in the world." Blues rhythms and blues sensibilities can be found in every character and in every speech—significant or not. He breathes blues into his characters and to listen to them can be rapturous. For Wilson, this is the song

10. Ibid., 49; emphasis added.

11. *Joe Turner*, 50.

12. Bill Moyers. "August Wilson: Playwright," *Conversations*, 1988, 63.

13. *Ma Rainey*, 66.

for the black American—it is the seed of redemption—as natural as breathing—as when God blew breath into the first human. Basic. Fundamental. We always had it. A part of our being. And when Herald Loomis finds his song he is "born again." When the characters in the Cycle find their songs, when they are redeemed, they are "born again." They have come home to the blues. They have found their identity.

When Wilson found Bessie Smith, it touched something that had always been in him (as in Ma's speech), but unexplored, and yet to be heard. He described the moment as "an epiphany: a birth, a baptism, and a redemption all rolled up into one."[14] He found the blues to be a "carrier of philosophical ideas for black Americans . . . their cultural response to the world."[15]

Blues and spirituals (a fundamental spiritual expression of the faith of people in deliverance from oppression) begin from the same place of suffering. Theologian James Cone believes that the blues and the spirituals are the same, except that the blues songs are secular—they confine themselves to the immediate.[16] The spirituals allude to the beyond, to deliverance. Cone says that blues is an artistic response to the chaos of life.[17] In that sense it harkens back to the metaphor of the Creation and breath, and now bringing order out of chaos, and in the process creating beauty—that which is not merely good, but *very good.*

What could be lovelier than finding that like the spiritual, the blues as well affirms life? Isn't that what Wilson intends in Ma's great speech when she says, "that's a way of understanding life"? Blues and spirituals start at the point of pain, then separate into secular and spiritual, and converge once more into a glorious affirmation of living—to glorify creation in all of its guises—to celebrate being. Africans in America could not have existed without the acknowledgment of suffering followed by the joy of hope. The blues is a testament to the resilience of the African-American spirit. Ma Rainey is right. The blues, "help you get up in the morning . . . knowing you ain't alone." This is what blacks uniquely brought to the American conversation—in music, in poetry, in prose—all as a way to come to terms with

14. Lahr, "Been Here and Gone."
15. Bigsby, "Interview with August Wilson," 208.
16. Cone, *Spirituals and the Blues*, 100.
17. Ibid., 103.

God; as a way of demanding to know as Levee bellows at the end, "where the hell was God when all of this was going on?"[18]

As the time for the recording session passes, and the reasons for the delays pile up, Ma's complaints multiply. It is too cold in the studio, her nephew, Sylvester, must recite the introduction (except that he has a very bad stutter, and it makes for several hilarious scenes—embarrassed audiences—but laughing-out-loud), and then when he finally gets it right (lots of applause), she stops and demands that Irving run down to the corner store for her "Coke Cola." She will not sing without it. She knows that this is iron-grip control, and she wields it. It's her only power to assure that she's treated with dignity. With fierce realism and unflinching gaze at the ugly truth, she says:

> They don't care nothing about me. All they want is my voice. Well, I done learned that, and they gonna treat me like I want to be treated no matter how much it hurt them. They back there now calling me all kinds of names . . . calling me everything but a child of God. But they can't do nothing else. They ain't got what they wanted yet. As soon as they get my voice down on them recording machines, then it's just like I'd be some whore and they roll over and put their pants on.[19]

She knows. She knows when her power is spent. And she will wield it as erratically as she damn well pleases. When the audience understands this, it loves her for it. It does not want her song to end. Nor does it want her sacrificed by the brash, young, foolish boy, Levee. Ma is the wise one, who has something to teach, to show. She knows about the song. She knows about redemption. She, like Aunt Ester, knows that when the ball is dropped you have to run back and pick it up. She is the repository of wisdom here. Indeed, she may have been the forerunner of Aunt Ester. She knows about how to be free, for she has not cast her future in the hope of the white man or the white man's God. Her freedom is planted firmly among the roots of her people, the beginning, the blues. It is where she finds her fulfillment, her sustenance, her power. The white man's world, and his God, hates her, uses her, and she is not fooled. She knows who she is. She is no nigger.

Levee. Wilson tells us that Levee is rakish, intelligent, and a buffoon[20]—a promising explosive combination that delivers. He is nonetheless

18. *Ma Rainey*, 80.

19. Ibid., 63.

20. Ibid., 14.

a musician of first rank and depth. Levee comes into the studio having lived a life, albeit short (he is in his early 30s), of rejections. He has been rejected and he rejects. He rejects the music style as Ma Rainey sings it and the band plays it. He has already arranged to have the band play it as he has contracted with the white studio owners to have it played. The band tells him that Ma is the boss, but Levee will have no part of it. He knows that he has cut a deal with the devil, and that suits him just fine, because the devil is in charge. That is okay with Levee because he has come to distrust God—the white man's God. Levee believes that the prayers to that God should be tossed into the garbage can. Herald Loomis's recoil at the mention of the Holy Ghost[21] strikes a similar chord and is a theme repeated in this play. Herald Loomis was snatched up by Joe Turner as he preached about that God and sent back into a captivity that was slavery for all intents and purposes. And he was trapped for seven years. For Herald Loomis, God and the enslavers were one and the same.

Cutler, arguably the most sensible member of the band, tells a story about a colored preacher who was stranded in an all-white town after sunset. The preacher wore a cross and carried a Bible. White men wanted to know what a nigger was doing in the town, and shot a gun to frighten the preacher, ripped the cross from around his neck, made the preacher dance, and told the preacher that it was a sin to dance with a Bible in his hand. They shredded the Bible with their bare hands. The colored preacher barely got out alive.

August Wilson is not alone in asking the fundamental question about what is the meaning of God's protection and love and mercy for the oppressed when confronted with gratuitous racial hatred and venomous white assaults to eviscerate blacks of all dignity. The question has been posed since the eighteenth century in America, when paternalistic conversions of slaves to Christianity were made. The same preachers who taught slaves to be good slaves and to obey their masters, else burn in Hell, led their white congregations to buy slaves in the hundreds.[22] Moreover, the irony of belief in that same God has queried, but by no means shaken nor shattered, the faith of eminent black theologians such as James Evans, Jr., Anthony J. Carter, and James H. Cone,[23] not to mention the witness of

21. *Joe Turner*, 50.

22. Spangler, *Virginians Reborn*, 52.

23. See, e.g., Carter, *On Being Black and Reformed*; Cone, *Black Theology of Liberation*; and Evans, *We Have Been Believers*.

faith of generations of black people in America. Nonetheless, as lovers of the blues, it is quite common to sing the blues as if God is irrelevant.[24] These slaves, however, had the presence of mind to hear the metaphor of liberation, both in the Hebrew Scriptures and in the story of the latter-day Moses, Jesus Christ—the savior, the redeemer, the comforter. There will be occasions in the Cycle when the language and the cadence of the blues will signal a return to God, and the evolution of a turn away from a state of alienation or separation or rejection. In *Radio Golf*, for example, Harmon Wilks's language takes on the unique rhythm of the Hill District as he has a reunion with his rich heritage. Here in the recitation of the story of the colored minister is the harbinger of a more sinister narrative to come—God's alienation with far more tragic consequences.

It is at the end of the first act that Levee explains something about his journey. His father in the South was frugal and saved money to buy some land. White men, full of envy, tried to rape Levee's mother. Levee, in an attempt to save her, was slashed deeply on the chest. His mother carried him to a white doctor, who refused to treat him, and she then carried him miles to a black doctor who saved his life. He almost died. His father then sold the land to one of those white men, killed one of them, and was lynched. Levee asked why God had not struck down those white people at that moment? Cutler and Toledo, representatives of the faithful and the white world, respectively, are offended and try to set Levee straight on his history and his legacy. Levee will have no part of it. Later, Ma fires Levee for his insubordination. Levee is unmoved since he has this side deal with the white owners. It is his fight with Cutler and Toledo that emerges as the key struggle in this drama.

Levee has understandably lost faith in the white man's God, who has all but abandoned his people and the people he loved. To what God does he pray? He and Herald Loomis have this in common. Yet, while Loomis finds redemption and freedom, Levee is not set free at all. He makes a reference to being lucky enough to come upon a devil who wants to buy up some souls. It is the first of a series of heretical thoughts that upset Cutler.[25] The irony is that Toledo agrees that the black man has sold his soul to white America—dressing like him, imitating him. Yet, it is Toledo who takes the fall for white America.

24. Cone, *Spirituals and the Blues*, 113.

25. *Ma Rainey*, 63.

When the banter returns to the colored minister who was harassed by white men with guns, and Levee asks where God was that he did not strike down those men right then and there—the unstated question being why doesn't God strike down these white men who force Ma to sing for her supper? But Levee doesn't comprehend that Ma has the upper hand. God has given her the blues to sing. Cutler, the faithful, tells Levee that he will burn in hell.

What follows is perhaps one of the most piercing speeches in English-speaking theater. It is a profane scream against God. And while we are spared the ritual baptism of a Loomis as in *Joe Turner,* we are not relieved of this injurious aural assault. It comes from Levee's memory of his mother's attempted rape and his father's lynching by a group of white men. He hears her voice when she called out for God's mercy, which was not present to protect her, him, the colored minister, or his father. He bellows:

> [H]e a white man's God . . . .God ain't never listened to no nigger's prayers . . . .God hate niggers! Hate them with all the fury in his heart. Jesus don't love you nigger! Jesus hate your black ass! Come talking that shit to me. Talking about burning in hell! God can kiss my ass . . . Your God ain't shit, Cutler.[26]

Few can hear that without some compassion for the lost soul who believes it, and who can say it. Yet, God matters to Levee. God matters enough that he can engender such a bilious eruption. The issue here is whose God is rejected. Like Herald Loomis's rejection of the Holy Ghost, this Levee has found that the God of the white man cannot speak to him. He needs to find his own God, his own song—not Ma's, not Cutler's, not Toledo's, but Levee's. But does he?

He goes on to threaten Cutler, but does not harm him. He spares him with an ominous warning and the brandishing of his knife that he will give Cutler's God a chance to "save his black ass."[27]

Levee suffers a rout. Ma fires him. The white studio owners sorely undervalue his arrangements (paying him five dollars a song)—all done in the company of the guys in the band. His humiliation is palpable. Toledo, whose literate pontifications have grated repeatedly on Levee, accidentally steps on Levee's new shoe, and as if Toledo represents the entire white race, Levee explodes in anger. In a flash, Levee's knife is out of its sheath and

26. Ibid., 80, 82.
27. Ibid., 81.

up to its hilt in Toledo's back. Toledo is dead. A horrific crime. He will be punished for it for a very long time.

Levee thus joins Wilson's group of "Warriors," those who fight—sometimes foolishly as Levee has just done, and who should and will pay dearly such a tragic mistake. He is like the others: Solly "Two Kings" in *Gem*, who freed slaves and who turned to helping abused factory workers; Herald Loomis; Boy Willie of *Piano Lesson* who has to fight off ghosts of the past to help his sister unlock herself; Floyd Barton of *Seven Guitars* who simply wants a future in music; Troy Maxson, of *Fences*, who battles death and the compulsion to save his son from racial humiliation; Sterling of *Two Trains* and *Radio Golf* who fights to redeem others; and King who gets sacrificed to redeem many in *Hedley II*.

Somehow August Wilson makes us love them. They long for God, although like Levee, they want to try to put a fence around this God, as if God can be easily defined—as this one for them and that one for us. Aunt Ester is a believer in God and supplements her longing for God with an abiding faith in the spiritual and mystical African world from which she came. We find ourselves wanting to help these warriors open their arms to embrace the broader traditions as embodied by Aunt Ester. When Citizen Barlow tells her that he has come to her to get his soul washed she says: "God the only one can wash people's souls. God got big forgiveness."[28] How I wish that Levee had been able to know Aunt Ester.

28. *Gem*, 20.

Arena Stage 2002 Production of *The Piano Lesson*,
with Harriet D. Foy. Photo by Scott Suchman.

CHAPTER IV

Mark That Day Down

The Piano Lesson
1936
Pittsburgh

The Piano Lesson[1] HAD already won the Pulitzer Prize by the time I had my first experience of it. It had been first produced at the Yale Rep in 1987, and had its Broadway opening in 1990. Then the prizes. I was prepared to be overwhelmed. I was not, and became increasingly annoyed as the evening wore on. The house was the cavernous Kennedy Center Eisenhower theater, my seat was near the left rear, there was no connection to the language or to the characters, and it was all too remote. No-fault-experience. For me, an evening or afternoon in an August Wilson world requires intimacy—an up-close relationship with the language. It is precise, it is luminous, it is beautiful, it is poetry. It would be many years later when I would discover *The Piano Lesson* for the first time and know its refinement, its joys, and its challenges.

This is the place where Wilson asks, what is your sense of self when you know your past, and yet you deny it? In the pilgrimage that takes place within the soul of Berniece Charles, the answer Wilson provides is quite simple. It is thwarted—thwarted by fear of the past's resonance. *The Piano Lesson* is the saga of how Berniece Charles comes to awaken, face, and accept that past. She is stuck at first, and cannot move beyond a barrier, but she later arrives to glorify whom she is, and is set free.

---

1. Wilson, *The Piano Lesson*, set in 1936.

The place is her Uncle Doaker's (her father's brother's) house. Doaker is a Pullman Porter and is gone from the home quite a bit. Berniece lives there with her eleven-year-old daughter, Maretha. There is an air of carefully crafted calm and order to the house. It is a portent. Disorder and turbulence are soon to arrive. The front parlor contains an upright piano, intricately carved like totems, with distinctive African motifs. The carvings are "rendered with a grace of power of invention that lifts them out of the realm of craftsmanship and into the realm of art."[2] There is a stairwell on the left of the stage leading to the second-floor bedrooms for Berniece and Maretha, while Doaker's room is on the right just off the front parlor. The center of the action is, as is the case with most Wilson plays, the kitchen—downstage and center.

Into this placid scene comes an early morning wake-the-dead pounding on the front door from Berniece's brother, Boy Willie and his friend Lymon—fresh up from the family home in Mississippi. Boy Willie's sunrise stormtrooper entrance and his exuberance upset the deliberately contrived order and serenity. With the first rap on the door, August Wilson has sounded the first essential thunderclap that will clear the stiff and prim household, and free Berniece of the inner ghost that enslaves her, and shackles her, and restrains her from redemption.

This is indeed the story about her journey to acknowledge her identity, to recognize when her day of freedom arrived, to know that she had already been redeemed by the mere knowledge of it. She is not distinguishable from Citizen Barlow, Herald Loomis, or Levee. They, each one, had who they were right there within their reach—their song was in their throats—they had to be guided to the soul's destination to sing it. Berniece has to find that day. She has denied it, and by so doing she never marked it down. She must visit it again and summon back the ancestors for help—she must play that piano—to embolden her, to help her remember. Wilson surprises us, for it is the seemingly shallow and destructive Boy Willie, full of bombast and hot air, who will be her great guide and warrior protector.

The notion of finding identity through song or music is the recurring melodic line throughout the Cycle. Solly and Aunt Ester sing in *Gem*, Bynum counsels Herald Loomis in *Joe Turner* to find his song, and of course Ma Rainey defines life itself by the blues songs she sings and hears in her heart. The brash and brilliant Levee sings it, but uses it as a cudgel. The song is the central metaphor in *Seven Guitars*. Wilson is a poet. And the

2. Ibid., The Setting.

real music is in his language—the spoken word—his lyrics. This play won the Pulitzer Prize for Drama and the NY Drama Critics Circle Award for Best Play.

The role of Boy Willie was deemed too challenging for the young actor Samuel L. Jackson during the early development in November 1987 at the Yale Rep. Thus, for Boston's Huntington Theater production in January 1988, Charles Dutton was given the Boy Willie role. And for his Broadway performance in 1990, he won the coveted Tony Award. This was also the big breakthrough for S. Epatha Merkerson as Berniece, who created the role on Broadway.

The Piano Lesson has density, texture, and heft. And because of its mystical overlay, some audiences find its meaning impenetrable and its refined and brilliant gifts too deeply buried to discern. While some dramatic segues may be slightly cumbersome (e.g., linking Berniece's ritual of straightening Maretha's hair to the piano story), once we return to the profound piano narrative of the family it is easy to forget a slightly bumpy ride along the way.

The Tension. Boy Willie wants to sell that piano. Berniece adamantly refuses to do so. Both Berniece and Boy Willie have equal and rightful claims to the piano—the equality of the claims they each acknowledge and respect. Their father brought it to the family home. Wilson gives their Uncle Doaker, the trustworthy narrator of sorts (an honest omniscient observer), the role of explaining the spiritual history and considerable emotional weight of the piano.

The piano did not belong to the Charles family at first. Far from it. In fact, it was an anniversary present from plantation owner Sutter to his wife, Miss Ophelia. The Sutters owned the Charles ancestors in slavery times. Old man Sutter bought the piano in exchange for one and a half slaves— Berniece and Boy Willie's great-grandmother Berniece and their nine year-old grandfather.

Although Miss Ophelia loved the piano and played it often, she missed having her two favorite slaves, Berniece and son, around with her. Sutter agreed to try to reverse the deal and get them back, but the dealer refused. Miss Ophelia, missing them so, began to waste away. That is when Sutter agreed to have Berniece and Boy Willie's great-grandfather, Willie Boy, come by and carve into the piano images of the traded slaves. That made Miss Ophelia happy.

But Willie Boy didn't stop with the two images. He continued to carve and craft likenesses of the entire family and their history, including "weddings" such as they were permitted, celebrations, generations—all intricately and lovingly carved into the piano. When Old Man Sutter discovered all of that he was furious. Miss Ophelia didn't care and continued to play the piano until the day she died; she liked the piano with its carvings because she had the piano and her "niggers too."[3]

Many years later, Boy Charles (Berniece and Boy Willie's father; Doaker's brother) decided that the piano, because of the ancestral labor and history, was rightfully and ethically his family's property. Thus, one 4th of July, while America was celebrating its freedom, Boy Charles decided to have a liberation day for his family as well. He took the piano from the descendant Sutter home, and set it in another county—presumably for safekeeping. The descendant Sutter, having discovered it missing, burned the Charles home as the prime suspect for its location, but no piano was in it. He later found Boy Charles (now on the run) in the boxcar of a train called the Yellow Dog, along with four hobos, and set it afire, killing all five men. From that day on, all suspicious murders in that county of Mississippi (including that of Sutter himself just days before the play begins) would be blamed on the retributive Ghosts of the Yellow Dog.

When the play opens Berniece has been living in Pittsburgh for three years following the death of her husband Crawley—a death for which she holds Boy Willie accountable—at least in part. She moved the piano to Pittsburgh with her. **Boy Willie wants to sell the piano because he needs the money to buy from Sutter the land on which the Charles family was held as slaves.** Berniece is not at all persuaded, and she is determined that the piano is not to be moved out of the house. Boy Willie is as insistent as she is stubborn. His attraction to that land is profound and rightly so. Berniece's need for that piano for which her father died, and that in hand-hewn labor and love tells their ancestral story, is equally as compelling. They cannot chop the piano in two—although Boy Willie has a moment or two when he suggests such a foolish idea. One is reminded of the King Solomon story of two "mothers" with a claim of right to a baby. Wise Solomon suggests splitting the baby in two, and one of the claimants agrees. She, of course, was not the real mother, whose love for her child would never countenance

3. Ibid., 44–46.

such a thing.[4] Boy Willie does not care about this piano. It lacks meaning for him, especially since Berniece never plays it.

Berniece. She cannot seem to go on living. It's been three years since Crawley (her husband) died, and it was as a widow that she came to Pittsburgh. She is still in mourning, stuck and unable to move on. There is no lack of male attention, however. There's Avery, a newly "called" minister who likes her and is even from down home in Mississippi. Wilson paints Avery as somewhat feckless and inconsequential—a useful portrait for the useless fight Avery wages against the threat of Sutter's ghost. The bottom line is that Berniece is just not that interested in Avery.

It's Lymon, who has arrived with the turbulence that is Boy Willie, who manages to quiet Berniece long enough to kiss her and make her feel like a woman again. His reach to her heart and his warming presence are signs— Wilson's dramatic devices—that Berniece is hearing the distant singing. Lymon, with the assuredness of a man who knows how to touch, anoints her with the perfume he's bought in hopes of finding a right woman. Right now, that woman is Berniece. She says nothing and does not stop him as he places dabs of the sweet liquid at her pulse-points, like that indented spot behind each of her ears. She turns her head slightly to make it easier for him to touch her there, behind her ears. It is her anointing for her re-birth—her baptism. It's Lymon who slows the pace, and with the cadence and lyrics of the blues he speaks. She listens:

> I woke up one time with this woman and I didn't know who she was. She was the prettiest woman I had ever seen in my life. I spent the whole night with her and didn't even know it. I had never taken the time to look at her. She must have known that cause she ain't wanted to see me no more.[5]

Ah, Wilson. I had this pretty woman, bedded her, she meant nothing to me, and she left; never wanted to see me again. Classic blues. Life, love, loss, survival. I moved on. He says this in response to her warning that he could get into trouble in the big city saloons—the implication being that he would be better suited to slowing down and dabbing her pulse points. Lymon's no fool. He may have taken a few detours on his pilgrimage to self-knowledge, but perhaps he's ready to come to rest now at the upright piano, seated on the bench next to Berniece.

4. 1 Kings 3:16–28 (JPS).
5. *Piano Lesson*, 78.

Berniece has not played the piano since her mother died. This is a big issue for Boy Willie. If she were playing it, then he would leave her alone about it, he says. As it is, it's just a piece of wood, merely a piece of furniture. She cannot bear to play it—to stir up the past. Her mother lived alone with it for seventeen years after her husband died in the Yellow Dog boxcar. She remembers with great sadness her mother's longing and grief. She may not be able to play it—to wake up the ghosts—but to sell the piano would be like selling her soul. She says:

> Mama Ola polished this piano with her tears for seventeen years. For seventeen years she rubbed on it till her hands bled. Then she rubbed the blood in . . . mixed it up with the rest of the blood on it. Every day that God breathed life into her body she rubbed and cleaned and polished and prayed over it.[6] . . . . I used to think them pictures came alive and walked through the house . . . . I said that wasn't gonna happen to me. I don't play that piano cause I don't want to wake them spirits. They never be walking around in this house.[7]

Her relationship to the piano is a complex one of resentment, denial, and respect for her ancestral heritage and fear. She resents that her father put himself in death's way by re-claiming the piano out of revenge for what old man Sutter had done to the family. The result, she bellows to her brother, was the series of seventeen years of loneliness for their mother and longing for a dead husband—all for a piece of wood—a piece of wood that is now a source of disharmony and discord in her home of apparent peace and order. And she wants—actually needs—to deny the ghosts of the past it resurrects.

This is Wilson at his dramatic best. Berniece is a cauldron of conflict; yet for dramatic effect, Wilson holds back critical information the audience needs to make a reasoned judgment about who is right in this battle of wills—Boy Willie or Berniece. Berniece is given the moral heft of the vision of seeing their mother rubbing the piano until her hands bled—raising the metaphor of blood drawn from the lash of slavery, from the toil of picking cotton, and of the soul's bleeding from being owned. Rubbing that blood into the wood is a powerful metaphor for holding on to what was sacrificed to keep it—even the blood of the man who retrieved it—the same blood of the woman who now wants to keep it.

6. Ibid., 53–54.
7. Ibid., 71.

Yet Berniece fears it. It is a past that holds her freedom and she cannot bear to face it—she cannot play that piano to awaken those spirits she wants to stay at rest. It's the spirits of the ancestors that she can sense are all about her already, and that is the information that Wilson has yet to disclose. There is one in particular who is especially awake and alive and threatening. He arrived just before the turbulent Boy Willie.

Boy Willie left Mississippi only days after Sutter died (or was pushed by Boy Willie, or perhaps the Ghosts of the Yellow Dog) by falling into a well. Boy Willie's Pittsburgh entrance was preceded by Sutter's ghost. It terrifies Berniece. Doaker has seen it but wisely refuses to confirm the visitation to Berniece. That would unsettle her. Profoundly so. And after Boy Willie arrives, Maretha is frightened by it. Sutter has come to retrieve his piano and is prepared to fight for it. Wilson establishes Sutter's ghost as the visitor who has come to redeem the vanquished honor of the enslaver—the one who would have the temerity to put God's children in shackles. When Berniece denies the presence, she enlivens it. And when Boy Willie blows in, her discomfort is magnified, for he insists that she face the spiritual past, even though that is never how he says it. He tells her to *honor* her past. He would also show her how to do that. Wilson crafts the liberation narrative—brilliantly.

Boy Willie. There is no comparable character to Boy Willie in any other August Wilson play, except the great Solly Two Kings in *Gem of the Ocean*. His first entrance is a whirlwind and is quickly tiresome.[8] Solly's presence is not disruptive in the Boy Willie style. Yet, they are each freedom fighters, in his own way. Boy Willie comes to Pittsburgh selling sweet Mississippi watermelons, ready to sell that old piano, take his half interest, then he is going back down home to buy back that Sutter land—the land on which the Charles family was enslaved. The land is available for sale because old man Sutter has died, and his son wants to sell the land.

Doaker quickly dismisses the idea of selling that piano, reinforcing what Berniece has already made quite clear. The piano will not leave the house. It will not be sold. Doaker repeats it as a refrain.

---

8. For sheer brashness, however, Boy Willie and Levee in *Ma Rainey* have much in common. Boy Willie is tiresome, but redeems himself by play's end. Some might complain that such an upbeat ending to *The Piano Lesson* is its dramatic failure. I disagree. Levee, on the other hand, is tiresome as well, but has a story that renders him quite sympathetic. Nonetheless, he commits a senseless murder and in the end for Levee, audiences hold little, or no, compassion.

Wilson gives Boy Willie a far more developed sense of identity and self-worth than Berniece's. Perhaps by having confronted Sutter and Sutter's son, his redemptive journey may have been already complete. The very fact of arriving proudly in an up-North city such as Pittsburgh with a barely-running old country truck full of the most stereotypical cargo two black men from the deep south can bring—watermelons, and lots of them; selling them to gullible northern white folks who buy their story that they're sweet because sugar has been put into the dirt—is a song of praise to blackness thrown as a big fat berry pie in a big white fat round face. Boy Willie has made a few bad choices over the years. He is, after all, one of the Wilson "warriors." When working in the lumberyards, he made some side deals to sell some of the wood he skimmed off the top. He got caught and went to jail for a time for it. He may have even pushed old man Sutter down that well. We don't know. Like other Wilson men, Boy Willie's mistakes have been bad, some not so smart—even stupid. But he's paid for them, he is struggling to walk around upright and is determined to do so. Boy Willie is no victim. He is a fully redeemed soul. He knows who he is and how he got to where he is. He knows his history; he has called on his ancestors; he knows on whose shoulders he stands; and he is comfortable and free. He remembers his past, and he engages it—like the children of Abraham, Isaac, and Jacob, who, as God directs, remember who delivered them. Boy Willie will have to fight freedom's enemy again—the Pharaoh's army, the men on horseback, the hunting dogs, the lynch mobs in hot pursuit—this time to free his sister from post-slavery bondage. Solly Two Kings was such a warrior, who could not rest until all of his people were as free as he had come to be, and put himself in harm's way to fight those ghosts of the past. Boy Willie wrestles with the ghost of his family's enslaver to free his sister—still in the family's old chains.

This day shall be to you one of remembrance: you shall celebrate it as a festival to the Lord throughout all the ages; you shall celebrate it as an institution for all time.[9]

Just family assembled—Doaker, Boy Willie, Berniece, and Maretha. Berniece presses Maretha's hair, using the fire from the kitchen stovetop for heat. Wilson has set the scene for Boy Willie to teach how essential it is that black people claim their identity, know their heritage, their struggles, their suffering and triumphs, how they got to where they are. This is a time of instruction—that the Charles family must understand what their ancestors

9. Exodus 12:14 (JPS).

did to get them to this place, and then summon them in celebration and gratitude for the sacrifice just as the Israelites are directed to call upon God in thankfulness for His redeeming them from slavery and delivering them from darkness to light—from the wilderness to Canaan—to the Promised Land, as he had promised to Abraham.

Berniece, impatient with Maretha who has just complained that her mother has hurt her in the hair-straightening process, snaps, "If you was a boy I wouldn't be going through this."[10] This is the opening. Boy Willie upbraids her and tells her that she should not make her daughter ashamed of who she is. She should make her proud, so that she can hold her head up, like telling her the story of the piano. The story of the piano—the story of how the family, by retrieving its accreted wooden implement of song (that metaphor of self), redeemed its freedom, its birthright. Wilson has him wax poetically:

> You ought to mark down on the calendar the day that Papa Boy Charles brought that piano into the house. You ought to mark that day down and draw a circle around it . . . and every year when it come up throw a party. Have a celebration. If you did that she wouldn't have no problem in life. She could walk around here with her head held high. I'm talking about a big party! Invite every-body! Mark that day down with a special meaning. That way she know where she at in the world.[11]

August Wilson often said that African Americans should celebrate the Emancipation Proclamation in the same way that Jews celebrate the Passover.[12] This beautiful Boy Willie speech is a Wilsonian ode to the idea that such ancestral knowledge—stripped away and shredded by slavery— is *truly redemptive*. It is also Wilson's clearest indication that Boy Willie has learned to embrace his history and heritage and is freed by it. The Boy Willie storm, for all of its tiresome tempestuous bombast, is the precise antidote for Berniece's stasis.

Sutter's Ghost. After Maretha's encounter with Sutter's ghost, Rev. Avery comes with biblical recitations to drive the ghost away. Its power is such that even the elaborate contraption that Boy Willie and Lymon have designed to move the piano will not work. The piano is now immovable. The confrontation is set.

10. *Piano Lesson*, 89.

11. Ibid., 90.

12. Moyers, "August Wilson: Playwright," *Conversations*, 74.

Questions abound. Avery's Christian incantations are no match for this ghost. Are they impotent, or must they be combined with African mysticism to counter the power of oppression? Perhaps it is only a human of African lineage, a descendant of slaves, who can defeat this enslaving presence who wants to hover and intimidate as a reminder of bondage.

It is only Boy Willie, this *particular* descendant of the enslaved ancestors, who can confront and defeat this force, this *special* enslaver, the captor, the owner of the human Charles chattel whose inherited wealth was earned on the backs of Boy Willie's grandfather and his grandfather's father and his father before him. Some have likened this to Jacob wrestling with the angel. Or perhaps more apt is the suggestion that it is black America wrestling with the legacy of slavery that can be driven away but never killed, and the wound of which never fully healed; no closure ever possible.[13]

Boy Willie goes up the stairs. Then there are sounds of a life-and-death struggle. He is fighting Sutter's ghost. Berniece knows now what she must do. Baptized and anointed by Lymon, she goes to the piano and begins to play. Her playing summons the spirits she long ago decided she did not want to awaken. She needs them now to help buy back her freedom. She needs them to enable, to protect, to defend, to empower her to move forward in her redemption journey. Boy Willie is doing all he can. But she must do something. She must get up and walk through the Red Sea; she must walk off the plantation; she must bleed for herself; she must get her soul washed; she must go to the City of Bones; she must run back for the ball should she drop it; she must walk to the great camp meeting, walk from Selma to Montgomery, from her home to register to vote, and get up on Election Day and pull the lever. Berniece must play the piano for herself and ask for and demand help. And that she does.

In a chant she repeats: "I want you to help me." Then she calls out names: "Mama Berniece . . . Mama Esther . . . Papa Boy Charles . . . Mama Ola." And over and over again, "I want you to help me."[14] Wilson's directions here are powerful. The song, he writes, "is both a commandment and a plea. With each repetition it gains strength. It is . . . an exorcism and a dressing for battle. A rustle of wind blowing across two continents."[15] The

13. Londre, "A Piano and its History," 119.

14. *Piano Lesson*, 105–6. August Wilson said that he often imagined audiences calling out names of their own ancestors at this point. Powerful sounds that. Summoning the ancestors—by name.

15. Ibid., 105.

spirit—always associated with wind—the epic battle between the souls of America and Africa.

There is the sound of a train that then subsides. It is intended as an allusion to the Yellow Dog and to Sutter's departure. Boy Willie leaves with a plea to Berniece to keep playing that piano—or else he (and maybe Sutter) will come back. Boy Willie's job is over. His sister's journey is complete. His family has been redeemed. Identity found. They know who they are. They know how they arrived. They will celebrate how it all happened, from this day forward. Alleluia.

Baltimore Center Stage 1997 Production of *Seven Guitars*,
with Clayton LeBouef, Leland Gantt, Russell Andrews and
Keith Randolph Smith. Photo by Richard Anderson.

CHAPTER V

They Come Down Out the Sky

Finding Redemption

in

Seven Guitars

PITTSBURGH. THE HILL DISTRICT. 1948. *Seven Guitars*.[1] Four men and three women—each of whom has a song to sing—seven variations on a blues theme of struggle, hope, ambition, and thwarted dreams. And in a surprising and unexpectedly tragic, twisted, and wrenching climax, two souls find their longed-for peace and redemption.

The central character is a talented blues singer named Floyd "School-boy" Barton. He is surrounded by a full-throated chorus—his girlfriend, Vera, and her friend and neighbor, Louise.[2] Louise's niece, Ruby, appears late in the first act. She's come from down south, pregnant we discover and in flight from man-trouble "with her little fast behind,"[3] as Louise insists on describing her. Ruby is physically lovely—sexy really, and a man-trap. Canewell is Floyd's sidekick and harmonica player, but he is also wise and is a counterweight to Floyd's occasional tendency to make bad decisions. Red Carter is also a Floyd colleague and a drummer. He maintains an independence from Floyd's dreams of musical greatness, yet he is all in when the work materializes. Hedley is a familiar type of Wilson character, a man

---

1. August Wilson, *Seven Guitars*, set in 1948.

2. Louise will live on in memory in *King Hedley II* as "Mama Louise," the then-deceased woman who acted as mother to Hedley II in infancy after Ruby departs to go on a singing career.

3. *Seven Guitars*, 56.

49

who occupies an interior world all his own, who exists in his own reality. He is not quite engaged on the same plane as those in the world around him. Some might describe him as being mentally challenged, yet he has found a comfortable niche, harmonizes well, and is not fearsome. Hedley raises chickens, harvests their eggs for sale as hard-boiled, slays and cooks them, makes chicken sandwiches, and sells them along with cigarettes and candy. He makes do with what he has. He has been coughing up blood, an indication that he is suffering from tuberculosis. Louise insists that he go to the doctor, but Hedley knows that they will put him into a sanitarium. He won't go; he does not trust white people to take care of him.

Out of these seven voices, the story of the tragedy is formed, and out of their singing the blues is a final act of redemption—for two.

Cy Morocco. *Seven Guitars* is one of the plays in which August Wilson gives full voice to one of his oracles—one of the people who exists in his own reality, is how I prefer to see it. Each of such Wilson's characters proclaims some truth. It was when I saw (and read) *How I Learned What I Learned* that I came to know that they are, in all likelihood, based on the life of a man Wilson knew as Cy Morocco.

Cy Morocco is featured in the play in various segments. On his own, he has been established as having lived in the Hill District and having known August Wilson and his friends. On occasion, he would approach people with an article from a magazine and say, "Hey, read this and see if you got what I got." The person would read it, and Cy would ask, "What did you get?" The person would answer, and Cy would respond, "Yes, that's what I got." As it turns out, Cy couldn't read, was too embarrassed to admit it, but in order to keep his dignity he adapted his own means of keeping informed. Eventually Cy lost his mind, and he knew it. He knew it, because he began to look for it and would ask people, "Have you seen it? I've got to find my mind," then go on about his way.

Wilson says in *How I Learned . . .* that Cy began to collect rocks and would present them to him as if it was "The Hope Diamond." Wilson says that he still keeps some of the rocks Cy gave him, and when one of his little girls would present him with a rock, it would remind him of Cy. "Cause I think they both know something that we don't." Seers are these characters for him. Oracles. Truth tellers. Knowing something that we don't. Solly

Two Kings,[4] Bynum,[5] Hedley,[6] Gabe,[7] Hambone,[8] Stool Pigeon,[9] and Elder Joseph Barlow[10]—seeing past, beyond, and through.

How it Began. Unlike with any other play in the Cycle, August Wilson spoke at length of how *Seven Guitars* began as an idea—an image. The image of the play came to him as four men, each playing a guitar—no women—in a turpentine camp in Georgia. But having no knowledge of turpentine camps[11] he moved the action to Chicago where he knew the blues would be at home. He also later realized that it needed the presence of women. First came Vera, who insisted on needing her own space. That turned out to be his mother's backyard in Pittsburgh. Thus the action was moved to Pittsburgh with Chicago as a place of dreams—a destination— perhaps an Eden or Paradise. When Vera entered, Wilson said, two women just came in behind her.[12]

Wilson saw himself as a collagist, taking his inspiration from Romare Bearden's "Mill Hand's Lunch Bucket" and "The Piano Lesson."[13] Wilson would routinely write speeches in long-hand and place them around his desk; I sense that they may have even been scattered at times. This would happen well before placing them in a narrative form of a story or play. The speeches were like songs—poems really. Later, they would find their way into the souls and voices of his characters. There were even times during the

---

4. *Gem of the Ocean.*

5. *Joe Turner's Come and Gone.*

6. *Seven Guitars.*

7. *Fences.*

8. *Two Trains Running.*

9. *King Hedley II.*

10. *Radio Golf.*

11. Turpentine camps were distilleries throughout the South in the early to mid-twentieth century. Black men distilled turpentine extracted from pine trees to be used as caulk to seal ships, in paints, for solvents, for ropes, and for medicinal purposes—all for menial wages—as little as $12 per month. Zora Neale Hurston wrote about the industry in the 1920s.

12. Murphy, "The Tragedy of *Seven Guitars*," 124–25.

13. See note 75, and Bigsby, "August Wilson: The Ground on which He Stood," 18–19. Romare Bearden was a twentieth-century African-American artist whose most famous works later in life (he died in 1988) were collages. They celebrated African-American rituals and everyday life. His artistic legacy has no peer, and now we can include August Wilson in the Bearden legacy. August Wilson wrote the foreword to the definitive study of Romare Bearden and his work. See, Myron Schwartzman, *Romare Bearden: His Life and Art.*

development of a play—perhaps while in rehearsal—that he would write a speech, often late at night, and give it to the dramaturge to find the "right" place for it in the play.[14] Thus, there were pieces, songs, poems, snatches of blues, guitar voices that needed to be harmonized (or not) into this narrative—this story. *Seven Guitars* has a resonance that it was created as a blend of voices and images to result in a painting, or more precisely a collage, of profound power and of sound.

The Voices. At the opening, four characters (Ruby and Hedley are not present) have just returned from the cemetery where they have buried Floyd "Schoolboy" Barton. Louise belts out a bawdy blues ballad inviting all to try her cabbage, and in a second verse gives a throaty few notes about how much the minister liked it, he shook with glee—so much that he gave her all the collection. Such affirmations of life at times of death can be keys to survival in tough times.[15]

Having argued over, and then devoured, the last slice of the sweet potato pie, they speak for the first time about the inexplicable at the grave. They all saw it. Six men in black hats arrived, seemingly out of nowhere, and carried Floyd up to the sky. Were they from the funeral home? There is some confusion. Vera is not confused. "They come down out the sky."[16] Whatever else has brought them to this moment, we know that Floyd has been returned to God—fully redeemed—worthy in the eyes of his Maker. How did we get here?

In a flashback, Floyd returns from having spent ninety days in jail for vagrancy.[17] Floyd hears the judge, and hears him clearly, who says to him that, "Rockefeller worth a million dollars and you ain't worth two cents . . .

14. Conversation with Todd Kreidler (August Wilson's last dramaturge), 18 October 2012.

15. Note 102, and see, e.g., Cone, *The Spirituals and the Blues*.

16. *Seven Guitars*, 9.

17. Vagrancy laws have been outlawed as unconstitutionally overbroad. After the 1865 emancipation virtually any freed slave (not under the protection of a white man) could be convicted of the crime. It was a part of a set of interlocking laws in the South (and elsewhere) designed to criminalize black life. The vagrancy laws were arbitrarily enforced as a means of controlling blacks. They were routinely rounded up off the streets for simply talking, not stepping aside when whites passed, or looking at whites directly in the eye. Having little, or no, money was evidence of worthlessness, establishing a *prima facie* case of being a vagrant. Wilson uses this set of laws as a means to emphasize how the larger society regarded black men as "worthless." See, Blackmon, *Slavery by Another Name*, esp. chaps. 2 and 5.

[t]hey took me down there and charged me with worthlessness."[18] Like many black men and women in America, Floyd struggles to find self-esteem in a society that does not take the time to pause for an adequate assessment of his (or any black man's) intelligence, creativity, worth, compassion, skill, or responsibility. Rather, it senses a black blur or takes a fleeting glance—long enough to sense danger or a threat to safety. At best, with the speed of a nervous tic merely deems him wholly dispensable and of no value whatsoever. It matters not what the judge actually intends; it is how his words pound upon Floyd's soul that matters. No value. No worth. He is then determined to make his value known in the world. He is determined to be whole again.

When each character speaks something of significance in *Seven Guitars*, the speech is a blues lyric. Floyd says he's in love with Vera, even though he ran out on her to Chicago with Pearl Brown a few years back. This is what he says to her:

> "That's the kind of woman a man kill somebody over." Then I see you turn and walk toward the door. I said, "They just gonna have to kill me." That's when I went after you. I said you was just right for me and if I could get that I never would want nothing else. That's why you ought to try me one more time. If you try me one more time, you never carry no regrets.[19]

That speech makes you swoon and exclaim, "sing to her, Floyd, sing to her!" Vera melts, of course. Who wouldn't? She has her moments of singing as well. They all do. She says to him:

> Floyd, I wanted to know where you was bruised at. So I could be a woman for you. So I could touch you there. So I could spread myself all over you and know that I was a woman . . . . You never showed me all those places where you were a man. You went to Pearl Brown and you showed her . . . I looked up and you was back here after I had given you up. After I had walked through an empty house for a year and a half looking for you. After I would lay myself out on that bed and search my body for your fingerprints. "He touched me here. Floyd touched me here and he touched me here and he touched me here and he kissed me here and he gave me here and he took me here and he ain't here he ain't here he ain't here quit looking for him cause he ain't here he's there! there! there! there!"[20]

18. *Seven Guitars*, 14.
19. Ibid., 17.
20. Ibid., 18.

A woman who loved with passion, lost, and now he is back, and wants her back. Her heart sings the blues, her mind tells her no, but her soul is stirring and longing to be back in his arms. And into that embrace is exactly where she goes, because that is where he wants her and where she needs to be.

Floyd had a hit record after he left the Army in World War II. It was "That's All Right." Like other black artists, he did not get royalties. He received a one-time payment, and if it became a hit, which it did, he had the possibility of signing a contract with a recording studio. Savoy Records in Chicago wants him to come to discuss the arrangements. Floyd has a letter. Mr. T. L. Hall, the insurance agent, has agreed to get it all in order with Savoy, but first Floyd has to get his money from the jail. It's his wages for being in the workhouse. He needs the cash to get his guitar from the pawnshop.

In an all-too-familiar refrain, the rules keep changing on him. He has an envelope to get his wages, but he also needs the letter. By the time he gets the letter and the cash, the time limit on the pawnshop redemption has expired by two days. The price to redeem his guitar has increased to beyond what he can now afford. Plus, he needs even more cash to make the Chicago deal work. The universe is working against him. Floyd is singing the blues.

Canewell and Red Carter are Floyd's pals. They are talented; they know their songs. They know the blues. Canewell likes Vera, even though Vera loves Floyd. Canewell is undeterred. He knows her to be a woman who knows about love—how to give it and how to receive it. Despite her disappointments, she does not live with regret. Canewell also knows how to turn a phrase. He says to Vera, "Some women make their bed up so high don't nobody know how to get to it. I know you ain't like that. You know how to make your bed up high and turn your lamp down low."[21] Canewell is also a fine musician. He can play the harmonica like it's "going out of style!"[22] Red Carter has been back-up drummer for Floyd for some time. Both Red and Canewell are realists and not dreamers, like Floyd. They may have been dreamers at one time, but age, humiliations, arrests for no apparent reason, and ambitions and hopes deferred and destroyed have made them practical men who appear to understand—and to accept—the limitations of their world. Neither is apparently unhappy in it, and although both men want Floyd to pursue his dreams of fame in music and love with Vera in Chicago, they have no desire to go there with him to live—only to make the recording, and then return home to Pittsburgh. Chicago is not an

---

21. Ibid., 93.

22. Ibid., Louise, 95.

Edenic destination for them. They struggle, of course. They are black men in 1948 America. Yet they seem to be content to be where they are in the sense that they do not hunger for much more. They know their songs. They know who they are. They have found their Redeemer, whoever or whatever it might be.[23]

Louise is similarly settled. She has known men and muses about her romantic past. She cautions Vera by recalling, in a "blues-y" way how one man in particular left her with only memories and a .38 caliber pistol. She says, "Don't let no man use you up and then talk about he gotta go. Shoot him first."[24] Louise is wise to meandering men and warns Vera about pouring herself into Floyd again. She knows, she observes, she sees, she's lived, and so she can sing the blues. They are the songs of truth—even if they can be the songs of mourning and a wail.

Ruby. Fast Ruby arrives from Birmingham. She's been sent north because her boyfriend, Elmore, shot and killed another man, Leroy, in a jealous rage. Leroy liked Ruby and she's carrying his child, although she's not sure if the father is Elmore or Leroy. She resolves that issue by having sex with Hedley, leading him and everyone else to believe that the child she has is Hedley's. She promises that if it's a boy she will name him King—King Hedley II.

Hedley makes the big journey in this play. He carries the heavy weights of the past that are his father's—whether accurate or not is irrelevant. To Hedley the facts are real enough to cause him enough pain to sit always on his chest. His deliverance comes in the form of taking Floyd's life in a case of mistaken identity. The mistake delivers Floyd from certain punishment and redeems Hedley. And in one dastardly, senseless, and violent act, each man is given a long-sought-after sense of worth.

We don't know why Hedley is captive in his own reality. He has the goal of having his father forgive him. The forgiveness will come when Buddy Bolden (a blues singer) will give him his father's money, and Hedley will be able to buy a big plantation, walk around it, and be a big man. His father's forgiveness will buy him freedom—a big plantation where the white man

23. Canewell re-emerges in the Cycle forty years later as Stool Pigeon in *King Hedley II*. He will be evolved into a sage about the history of the black people in America, and a student of Aunt Ester's wisdom. Forty years later, he will have become one of Wilson's oracles—spouting biblical wisdom, that has no biblical basis, but is only partly grounded in Yoruban custom and tradition. His Stool Pigeon name will be derived from his disclosure to law enforcement the identity of Floyd's murderer here, in *Seven Guitars*.

24. *Seven Guitars*, 34.

won't be able to tell him what to do anymore. Hedley is that metaphor here for black liberation and redemption, as blacks in America know their own reality and identity—independent of the white culture. Hedley is about to become another "Wilson warrior"—making mistakes, sometimes big mistakes, and paying dearly for them, but in the process achieving a sense of freedom and stepping onto Higher Ground.

Hedley's independence is land-based. It is the type of freedom that cannot be taken away. Much like the celebration of the mythic value of land as expressed by Boy Willie in *The Piano Lesson*, ownership of land in America lessens significantly the possibility that white people will deprive you of basic freedoms.[25] He celebrates the kingdom of Ethiopia, the promise of Marcus Garvey as a proclaimer of black man as king.[26]

Hedley killed a man because, he says, he refused to call him a king as his father had called Buddy Bolden. Hedley wants to sire a son who is a messiah. Although the external world regards him as odd, Hedley is really quite comfortable. "Like Jesus Christ was a big man . . . Maybe Hedley never going to be big like that. But for himself inside. That place where you live your own special life. I would be happy to be big there."[27] The lesson Wilson teaches here is that real and true serenity and freedom are inside and not dependent upon outside affirmation. Each person must take the individual journey to redemption and to freedom, and must find his own song, his own identity.

Hedley shares all of these intimate thoughts, dreams actually, with Floyd. Floyd patronizes him with assurances that Buddy Bolden will bring him his money—enough to buy two plantations. Floyd's deception is minor. Ruby's lie will resonate for the next forty years, and she will live to pay the price for it. She dupes Hedley into believing that the child she carries is his son. Hedley II will almost make it to his grave believing it to be true.

Floyd just cannot seem to get a break. His World War II Adjustment Pay was $47.00. That was enough for him to slip away to Chicago with Pearl Brown, and to record "That's All Right," the hit song. Chicago was expensive, and although he received a single payment for the record, he had no manager, and thus had no way of making it financially. Upon his eventual and

25. Subsequent stories of urban renewal and gentrification of the Hill District will test these theories. The theories by this time were also stripped of much validity on the world stage throughout Africa as the Europeans colonized many countries.

26. Marcus Garvey was a heroic figure who lived in Harlem in the 1930s and led a "Back to Africa" movement. It took on mythical status in parts of black America.

27 *Seven Guitars*, 65.

inevitable return to Pittsburgh, he met T. L. Hall, who represented himself as a manager, and who doubled as an insurance agent. Floyd's arrest, conviction, and jail term for vagrancy delayed his plans to go back to Chicago with T. L. Hall. After release from jail, he needed the cash from his incarceration to redeem his guitar from the pawnshop, now delayed because of red tape, and the delay resulted in the increased redeemed price on the guitar. He got a letter from Savoy records in Chicago indicating a willingness to discuss a recording contract and gave Hall his money to follow up with Savoy. Hall, we soon discover, has been arrested for writing fraudulent insurance policies. Hall has taken all of Floyd's money. It's all gone. No money. No guitar. No way of getting to Chicago. Dreams dashed. How is he to be delivered?

Floyd then makes the big mistake. Together with Poochie, the neighbor's son, they rob a bank. A cop kills Poochie as he runs to make a clean get-away. Floyd disappears for a few days. No one suspects him as being a part of the crime. He returns with a new guitar, a dress for Vera, and two tickets to Chicago—one for Vera and one for himself. When no one is looking he buries the remaining cash in Hedley's garden. The whole group goes to the club for a jam session—Floyd, Red, and Canewell on the stage with Vera, Louise, and Ruby in the audience. The evening is a triumph.

Later, Canewell poking about in the garden discovers the money, and he and Floyd have an argument about who has the greater right to it. Canewell quickly realizes that the cash is from the bank robbery and backs away immediately.

As soon as Floyd is alone, Hedley sees him holding all of this money. Hedley is confused at first, and then he comes quickly to believe that the money is the realization of his father's promise to deliver cash through Buddy Bolden. He tries to take it from Floyd and they scuffle. Hedley imagines that Floyd is trying to take away his father's cash—trying to steal his freedom, his birthright, and he must fight for it. After Floyd knocks Hedley to the ground, Hedley gets up and exits. He returns with a machete. Without hesitation and with a smooth movement, Hedley slashes Floyd's throat. An honorable mistake, but a mistake—a tragic mistake nonetheless. Hedley is freed, redeemed. In his reality, he has not permitted his birthright to be stolen. There will be no Esau for Hedley. Esau has been redeemed. This ritualistic slashing is also resonant of Herald Loomis's redeeming sacrifice of blood in *Joe Turner*,[28] this concept that in redemption and liberation it is essential to shed blood.

28. *Joe Turner*, "I don't need nobody to bleed for me! I can bleed for myself"; 85–86.

The poignant twist is that Floyd's blood is sacrificed in this ritual of redemption, for he too, in the larger reality beyond Hedley's interior world, is free at long last of the woe and the weight of worthlessness—the freedom he never found within. For all of the struggles he had lived, endured, and survived, there was the most painful—systematically underestimated and undervalued by the dominant culture—worthless. A black man. Now redeemed. But there's more. At the cemetery, those six men in black hats that came down from the sky and raised him right up—took him right up to heaven. Earth may have found no value in him, but God loved him and took him Home. Worthless no more. As the people sing:

> Soon Ah will be done with the
> troubles of the world
> The troubles of the world
> The troubles of the world
> Soon Ah will be done with the
> troubles of the world
> Goin' home to live with God[29]

---

29. Negro Spiritual, circa nineteenth century.

Arena Stage 1990 Production of *Fences*, with Yaphet Kotto,
Kim Hamilton, and Wally Taylor. Photo by Joan Marcus.

CHAPTER VI

Banish Them with Forgiveness

Fences

1957

> *When the sins of our fathers visit us*
> *We do not have to play host.*
> *We can banish them with forgiveness*
> *As God, in His Largeness and His Laws.*[1]

FORGIVENESS. WITHOUT IT WE would weep for this man and the abandoned and lonely life he came to. As it is he needs all of our compassion and our love. And he gets it. What is it about this Troy Maxson, who seems to tower above all of Aunt Ester's children—in his mix of power, threat, capacity for love, disgusting and frustrating limitations, selfishness—that compels us to love him in spite of it all, to feel the urge to push his wife and son to forget his intentional cruelties, and to forgive him? Is it because we know that the bitterness for them is self-corrosive? That forgiveness is best for them? Or has Wilson written so compellingly of this man that we peer into a soul of wonder and care and need? We can come away from an experience with Troy Maxson and be completely bewildered by why we are mourning his death—this infidel, this bully of a father who with cruelty limits his son's ambitions.

Troy Maxson is a Wilson Warrior.[2] Like the others, he takes a journey—a pilgrimage—a pilgrimage (for there is in fact a spiritual destination)

---

1. August Wilson, Prologue to *Fences*, set in 1957.

2. Solly Two Kings in *Gem*; Herald Loomis in *Joe Turner*; Levee in *Ma Rainey*; Berniece and Boy Willie in *The Piano Lesson*; Floyd "Schoolboy" Barton in *Seven Guitars*;

of redemption to find and to reconstitute who they might have been, and what they have become. And in so doing they must have the strength and the courage—the faith—to revisit the past, in all of its several guises and heaviness, to set down the burdens of that past, and become free. The faith is needed to know that the outcome will be as God intends, despite the difficulties attendant to the journey. These men (and Berniece Charles) are warriors in fact, and not merely in spirit (but certainly in that as well), and have that Warrior courage. They make mistakes. Bad mistakes. They pay the price for them. Yet, they are not victims. They are fighters.

In a slight twist on the customary Wilson narrative, in *Fences* it is a woman—it is Rose who takes on the primary role of conducting the redemptive journey of forgiveness for the men around her.[3] Rose leads them through their wilderness. Rose is the Pillar of Fire by night and the Pillar of Cloud by day. Troy's wife and Cory's mother, Rose convinces the men to drop the stony weights of their fathers' burdens, and find their freedom and fulfillment right where they have been led. Steadfast Rose.

Troy Maxson, however, is the aptly named large presence here—dominating, physically talented, looming, and limited. Troy is illiterate. His challenges are inter-generational, and he carries resentments against his own father on his back like his father carried bales of cotton. His father was an Alabama sharecropper, who of course came to know that no matter how much he produced, always found himself in debt at harvest time. In a riveting speech about how he had to leave Alabama, Troy speaks of making love to his girlfriend and discovering that his daddy was watching; he wanted her as well. They fought over her. The only thing Troy remembered was trying to get up from the ground with one eye swollen shut. He had to go because he "could feel [his daddy] kicking in [his] blood and knew that the only thing that separated [them] was the matter of a few years."[4] They were just alike. They wanted the same things out of life. They could no longer occupy the same space. It was time. Troy walked away. It was a rite of passage.

Sterling in *Two Trains Running*; Booster in *Jitney*; King in *King Hedley II*; and Harmond in *Radio Golf*.

3. Aunt Ester does not even receive a mention until *Two Trains Running*, in which she is a presence and a force, but not an on-stage character. And even though she takes on the primary redeemer role in the Cycle in *Gem*, chronologically *Gem* was the penultimate play written among the ten. *Fences* preceded *Gem* by eighteen years. Rose, a woman, as redeemer was, in that sense, a Cycle "pioneer."

4. *Fences*, 50.

The same ritual of departure (or ejection) would be repeated years later when Troy's own son, Cory, would fight for the same space inside the same fence, and his father would vanquish him. Cory, too, would have to go. They would want the same things out of life, and they would not be able to find them and be free in the same yard.

Rose would understand and let go. She would allow her son to go beyond the fence. And just as Troy Maxson would eventually find compassion and forgiveness for his own father, Cory would realize that to know peace and freedom he would have to forgive Troy, as well. His mother Rose will sing the blues to him, and lead him there—a soul redeemed.

After Troy arrived in Pittsburgh from Alabama, he supported his young wife and new son, Lyons, with a life of crime. He spent fifteen years in jail for armed robbery, and while there he learned to play baseball. And he played it with such talent and skill that he became known as one of the best Negro players in America. He chafed at the limited category—he was one of the top players, *period*—white or black. By the time he was released, his marriage was over; he was too old to pierce the top tier of the baseball leagues, and especially the newly integrated professional leagues.

We meet him when he is fifty-three, earning his living as a garbage man, married for eighteen years to the ever so solid and faithful Rose. Their seventeen-year-old son, Cory, is a good student and a talented athlete at football, while holding an after-school job as a bagger at the local A&P grocery store. Wilson writes Cory to have no outward flaws—he makes everybody proud—"Wheaties box" style. Cory is thus perceived to be all the more sympathetic in the cage of Troy's harsh and unreasonable limits. Troy's older son, Lyons, comes around regularly (predictably on Troy's payday) to borrow cash. Troy subjects him to the obligatory humiliation, while Rose accepts Lyons unconditionally, as she does with all aspects of her life with Troy.

Anchoring Troy from outside the fence of family is his friend and coworker, Bono. Troy and Bono became buddies in jail. They work together on the garbage truck. Bono is kind, loves Troy, tells him so, and respects him and what he has built with Rose as a family unit. Bono and his wife are seemingly happily married. Bono and Troy are tight. Such male bonding is not uncommon for the 1950s. What is remarkable is Bono's comfort in expressing his love and admiration for Troy—rare in buttoned-down mid-twentieth-century America—black hyper-masculinity America. Wilson wants us to know then that Bono means it. Bono will prop up Troy on his "every leaning side." That is a very big deal. Bono proves it. He speaks up when he knows that Troy is betraying Rose. He becomes Jonah to Troy. He tells Troy to get up, turn about, repent, or face destruction of all he has. He lays it all out. Rose is a good woman and a fine wife. Troy minimizes Bono's warnings, even denies them.

Of course, Wilson's Troy Max-son is a big man physically. A strong man. He describes him as "a large man with thick, heavy hands; it is this largeness that he strives to fill out and make an accommodation with. Together with his blackness, his largeness informs his sensibilities and the choices he has made in his life."[5] Troy seeks to "fill out" his space, his potential, and the goals he feels he has never achieved. He was never able to get into the baseball big leagues because he was too old. He doesn't think this is at all true. He knows it is because he is black. No one can convince him otherwise. His statistics surpassed the best of the best. Race tells only part of the story. Bono and Rose tell him that he simply came along too early.[6] He speaks of his other frustrations and disappointments. Or are they simply failures? He wanted to provide a home for his family, yet the only way he could afford to purchase the house was through the funds from the military. They paid damages to his brother, Gabriel. The damages were part of the recovery for head injuries Gabriel sustained in World War II that blew away part of his skull. The consequence was that Gabriel was left mentally and physically impaired. No fulfillment there.

There are ways, however, that he believes he can be fulfilled. He is willing to fight for them. He thinks he can control who and what enters his space, whether it is staving off the inevitable disappointment his son will face from rejection by the sports world, or the persistent repeat encroachment of Death from a too-early visit—a visitor he is determined to fight on his own terms from inside his own space, his own fence. He does *not* believe that the sports world will give his black son a fair chance and does not want Cory to be hurt. Troy thinks that Cory will be exploited and left with nothing. August Wilson thinks that Troy is right to keep Cory away from the exploitative world of sports—the world that devours black men. It puts them in college solely to be in the athletic arenas, and they get no education.[7]

---

5. Ibid., 9.

6. Ibid., 16.

7. Savran, "August Wilson: 1987," 32.

Cory rearranges his after-school job to make room for football practice in his schedule, in direct defiance of Troy's orders. Troy reverses all of Cory's moves—the result is a furious and frustrated Cory. Rose calmly says to Troy that he should let the boy play football.

For a while Troy thinks that he can stand up to death, although he knows that death is nothing to play with. Full of bluster he declares that he "ain't worried about death . . . all death is to me is a fastball on the outside corner."[8] It has haunted him, and it almost took him some years back, but Troy fought it, and won. As the narrative progresses, what appears to come into focus is that only death will free Troy of his weights—his sheer size of a being that becomes too awkward for him to carry. The progression for Troy—his journey, and why we have such compassion for him—is that he will fight to carry on, yet his life paradoxically has decreasing purpose, because he is increasingly unfulfilled by the love of those around him.

Yet and still there are expectations—that he would fill out the spaces and the corners inside the fence. Rose had large, empty spaces for which she needed him. She knew he was big enough for her to be "filled to bursting."[9] Cory needed not merely to be provided for—he needed to be *loved* by his father—to be shown that love, *demonstrably*. In a 1950s-style male-repressed and reticent exchange, Cory, as a teenage boy would not mention the "soft" word, love, but having been sternly upbraided by Troy that he must not (will not) pursue that football scholarship, but will keep that grocery store job instead, Cory asks, practically trembling with fear, "How come you ain't never liked me?"[10] Troy cannot. No. Will not. Troy will not satisfy Cory's desperate longing. And in a cruel and staccato-like series of buckshot-loaded questions about whether Cory has clothes on his back, a bed to sleep in, a roof over his head, if he eats every day, Troy then says that any question about liking him makes him a fool. He provides for him, says Troy, not because he likes him, but because it is his job to do so. Cory is the dismissed with, "I ain't got to like you . . . You understand what I'm saying boy? Then get the hell out of my face . . . ."[11] As Tennessee Williams's Blanche says, "Deliberate cruelty is not forgivable. It is the one unforgivable thing in my opinion."[12] I couldn't agree more. Poor Cory,

---

8. *Fences*, 17.

9. Ibid., 88.

10. Ibid., 38.

11. Ibid., 39.

12. Williams, *A Streetcar Named Desire*, scene 10.

having to withstand this onslaught. And it is later said by Rose that Cory wanted to be just like his father. Really?

Provision by a father for his children is never to be regarded merely as a duty, but as an act of love. Any dialogue about it must never be taken as an affront as Troy assumes it is here. By his attack upon his son, Troy Maxson has now shifted the burden of proof, and must now demonstrate that he is now not only worthy of his child's love, but also of his respect. He does not do so. Rose has to lead Cory to the place of big forgiveness.

Big Troy. Large man with large needs. He craves fulfillment within and outside that fence. He'll not find it. Although he knows that death will ultimately win, he will give it quite the struggle and will swing at it one last time. Troy believes that he's been cheated out of life. He cannot be filled up at home; consequently he lacks the capacity to satisfy the longings of those who crave his love.

Sing Him Home. Troy knows what is constant and true. He has a steady job on the trash truck, and at his prodding he gets a promotion from hauler to driver. His co-worker and steady pal, Bono is loyal, satisfied, not especially ambitious, sensible, earth-bound. Yet Bono's two feet on the ground don't keep him from singing the blues as if he's calling up to heaven when it's time. Wilson imbues Bono with that gift of song when Troy says to Bono that he bets Bono never disobeyed his daddy. Bono says (this time speaking to Lyons—it's payday so Lyons is about):

> I ain't never had a chance. My daddy came on through . . . but I ain't never knew him to see him . . . or what he had on his mind or where he went. Just moving on through. Searching out the New Land. That's what the old folks used to call it. See a fellow moving around from place to place . . . woman to woman . . . called it searching out the New Land. I can't say if he ever found it. I come along, didn't want no kids. Didn't know if I was gonna be in one place long enough to fix on them right as their daddy. I figured I was going searching too. As it turned out I been hooked up with Lucille near about as long as your daddy been with Rose.[13]

Call it blues, call it poetry, call it prose. It is an aria. And it is an aria and an ode to honest, faithful, and steadfast love that's just okay. It is the kind of sweet little aria that keeps the action moving, and that can be so lovingly extracted from the whole opera. Most people after a while might even forget the opera from which it came, the character who sings

---

13. *Fences*, 48.

it, because they fell in love with it so long ago, just as it is—standing so sweetly and perfectly, all on its own. And as is the custom with the blues, while it acknowledges life's hardships and woes, it affirms life. Yes, Bono proves his love to Lucille and to the Maxson family, but especially to Troy. He is yet one other person needing to be fulfilled by, and wanting to fulfill, Troy Maxson. And it is Bono who sees Troy's destructive attraction to some "Alberta gal," and the threat to Rose.

Gabriel, the oracle character in *Fences*, is the looming presence of truth for Troy, both past and future. Gabe doesn't intend it, but pulls back Troy's veil of illusion. He speaks of what he sees, and what he sees is his vision of the unvarnished truth. Wracked by guilt when Gabriel makes his unexpected and, for Troy, unwelcome appearances, Gabriel compounds the ache by being true to his divine function. He tells of seeing Troy's name in St. Peter's book. He can see Rose's, too, but not like Troy's—he can *really* see Troy's. "How many times you gonna tell me that Gabe?"[14] Troy can't get angry, perhaps slightly peeved, but not mad; Gabe cannot help himself. Troy and family basically live in Gabe's house, but Gabe desiring some independence moved out and lives with Miss Pearl. True to his name, he carries a trumpet, ready to blow when St. Peter orders him to open the gates of heaven for Troy, specifically, and for the Judgment, in general. But in the meantime, he sells small items like fruits and such and chases the occasional fearsome "Hellhounds" away. But each time he appears, Troy cannot get away fast enough, it seems. He squirms. His discomfort is worn like a tight shirt, ready to pop its buttons. Yet Rose loves Gabriel, and as with everyone who happens by, she offers food and a kind word and welcome. Rose is a sanctuary. Calm. Peaceful. She puts people at ease and provides sustenance. She feeds them. She protects them from irrational outbursts. She manages to insure that they get what they need. Lyons comes by to borrow money; Troy resists; Rose facilitates. Each time. She is a Divine Presence in the midst of chaos. If they love Troy; she loves them. It's clear.

Troy, on the other hand, is a man who is perplexed by a life that is not enough. Was he inspired by that 1979 encounter that Wilson had in the Hill District with an old man, who called him Youngblood?[15] The old man said to Wilson:

> See . . . you going through life carrying a ten-gallon bucket. And if
> you go through life carrying a ten-gallon bucket, you always going

14. Ibid., 29.
15. "Youngblood" will appear as the youngest character in *Jitney*. See chapter VIII.

to be disappointed. Cause it ain't never going to be filled . . . Don't
you go through life carrying no ten-gallon bucket. Get you a little
cup and carry that through life. And that way somebody put a little
bit in it and then you have something.[16]

Troy is trying in vain to fill that big bucket, and he just cannot do it. No one
in his life can help him do it. It's just not enough. And like Wilson himself,
getting it all down to a cup—no way. Troy deserves better.

He is spent. He gives all he knows how to give, and Cory wants more;
Rose wants more. He is trapped inside the fence. A signature speech sings
the blues of his frustration and woe, and he tells/sings it to Rose as a way
of explaining the inexcusable. And although we ache with gut-wrenching
compassion for Rose when he tells her that Alberta is pregnant with his
child, we understand why he ventured beyond the gate. This is what he says:

> Woman . . . I do the best I can do. I come in here every Friday. I
> carry a sack of potatoes and a bucket of lard. You all line up at the
> door with your hands out. I give you the lint from my pockets. I
> give you my sweat and my blood. I ain't got no tears. I done spent
> them. We go upstairs in that room at night . . . and I fall down on
> you and try to blast a hole into forever. I get up on Monday morn-
> ing . . . find my lunch on the table. I go out. Make my way. Find my
> strength to carry me through the next Friday. *(Pause)* That's all I
> got, Rose. That's all I got to give. I can't give nothing else.[17]

Whatever he has at home is not enough to fill him up. The rest of his
needs are somewhere else, and that is where he can sing his song and laugh.
And he needs to sing it before death comes. He has found that he can be
with Alberta and, as he tells Rose, "laugh out loud . . . and it feels good. It
reaches all the way down to the bottom of my shoes."[18]

That leaves Rose to wail and to find a way to live with the shock of betrayal, unfaithfulness, and misplaced trust. She makes sure that he knows,
in yet another powerful speech, that as her inevitable doubts arose over
their eighteen years together, she learned to hold on tighter, and to bury her
doubts inside him. He reacts with a series of baseball metaphors. She's had

---

16. Wilson (with Kreidler), *How I Learned What I Learned* (unpublished manuscript,
October 2014). Wilson's response was that he's been trying to cut it down to one-gallon.
He would never get it down to a cup. He "deserves more than that," 56–57. See also West's
advice to Sterling in *Two Trains Running*, 85.

17. *Fences*, 40.

18. Ibid., 65.

enough, and brings him right back with, "We're not talking about baseball! We're talking about you going off to lay in bed with another woman . . . "[19] When she reaches a climax of emotion and pain, she throws her head back and says to him that he takes without knowing how much has been given. His resentment at being told that he doesn't give makes him take out after her. Cory enters and mistakes all of this as his mother in physical danger. He takes up the ritual Oedipal struggle with his father, who wins with Cory flat on the ground. Troy warns him that this is his "Strike Two." One more before he strikes out.

This is majestic. It is opera. It is blues opera. The voices are strong, peerless, pitch-perfect, and a well-tuned ear cannot miss the transcendent rhapsodies. Wilson said that this is his least favorite play. He wrote it in response to those who insisted that he needed something in the genre that contained a nuclear family and was "more accessible."[20] Whatever the reason, the speeches/songs/lyrics of dialogue between Rose and Troy upon the disclosure of his betrayal are among the most beautiful, poignant, and powerful in all of the Century Cycle.

If Troy's bigness overwhelms, it is in stark contrast months later. He is diminished, minimized. He has given written permission to have Gabe locked up as a danger to the community when he chases away "Hellhounds." Troy did not intend to have Gabe locked up. He didn't understand what he signed. Troy is illiterate. Not so large. Not so big. Pitiful, actually. He's of a size now that death can have at him.

The final struggle with Cory comes in the form of Cory's failed effort to hit his father with a baseball bat. And for that Cory is told that he's "just another nigger in the street,"[21] and that his things would be found outside the fence.[22] August Wilson sees this as Cory's "rite of passage"[23]—a necessary ritual, almost as if to earn Troy's respect, to become a man himself. It is the fight, of course, that Troy had with his own father and Troy—van-

---

19. Ibid., 66.

20. Watlington, "Hurdling Fences," 88.

21. This is a line that would be uttered by Becker to his son, Booster, on the occasion of their reunion after Booster's release from prison, having served a twenty-year term. See, *Jitney*, 46. Chapter VIII. The two had not spoken to, or seen one another, for that entire time. It is a profound statement on the complexity of father/son alienation that has its ancient roots in the infanticidal story of Abraham's sacrifice of Isaac. See Genesis 22:9–10 (JPS).

22. *Fences*, 81.

23. Sheppard, "August Wilson: An Interview," 112–13.

quished, simply picked himself up and walked away to be in Pittsburgh. Troy did not find his song at his first stop in Pittsburgh. Likewise, Cory will not find his song of redemption at his first stop in the Marines. He will have to come back home again and hear first from his mother, Rose—his pillar of fire.

The big dramatic test for Rose is Alberta's death in childbirth and Troy's arrival at home with his newborn daughter, Raynell—motherless. Rose agrees to take care of the innocent child because, "a motherless child has got a hard time," she adds, to Troy, "from right now . . . this child got a mother. But you a womanless man."[24] It never fails that the audience roars its approval.

Troy dies in 1965. Raynell, the daughter, is 7. Cory is 24. Lyons is 41. Each of Troy's issue is equidistant in age—17 years apart. A generation each. They have gathered for his funeral. Bono, of course, steadfastly loyal in love to the end, offers to go to the church to get the pallbearers all lined up. Lyons is on release from jail to go the funeral. He's been locked up for cashing other people's checks. Cory is erect and perfect in his corporal rank Marine uniform. All are making great big fuss about how he's made something of himself, and how they all knew he would. Rose is especially happy to see him, of course. Cory and Raynell are getting to know each other. She tells him that she sleeps in what her daddy calls "Cory's room." This is Wilson's device to assure us of Troy's enduring love and respect for Cory, and of his determination to keep his spirit alive in the home. Rose tells us how Troy died. It was one last swing of the bat, of course. Just as Troy would have it. His time of redemption and fulfillment came, but he would need Gabriel to finish the job for him.

Rose now needs to help her son free himself from the pain of the past. He tells her that he won't go to his father's funeral. Rose goes to work. She is this story's Aunt Ester—the deliverer, the redeemer, the comforter. She embodies now, Rose does, all that is essential—the mystical, the spiritual, the religious—and all that surrounds to protect and to guide. She says, sings, "Whatever was between you and your daddy . . . the time has come to put it aside. Just take it and set it over there on the shelf and forget about it . . . You got to find a way to come into your own. Not going to your daddy's funeral ain't gonna make you a man."[25]

24. *Fences*, 74.

25. Ibid., 87. This is advice that Aunt Ester dispenses to Sterling, as he reports in *Radio Golf*. He had old pains and self-pity from being an orphan, and she advised him to

Cory responds with the truth of how ominous his father's being had been. "Papa was like a shadow that followed everywhere. It weighed on you and sunk into your flesh. It would wrap around you and lay there until you couldn't tell which one was you anymore . . . Everywhere I looked Troy was staring back at me . . . I've got to find a way to get rid of that shadow."[26]

Rose helps him to understand that only he can find the means of freeing himself from the weight of that shadow. She simply says that the shadow was Cory. It was Cory, who like Troy, was growing into himself. All sons must learn to cut that shadow down to fit themselves, or to grow into it. And in so doing, to forgive their fathers. To become themselves—to become free—to be redeemed. She says, "that's all you got to measure yourself against the world out there. Your daddy wanted you to be everything he wasn't . . . and at the same time he tried to make you everything he was. I don't know if he was right or wrong . . . but I do know he meant to do more good than he meant to do harm. He wasn't always right. Sometimes when he touched he bruised."[27]

Then Cory and Raynell—two siblings—joined by the blues their daddy taught them, sing a song about an old dog named Blue that ends with old Blue's death. Blue is now treeing possums in the Promised Land. The old dog that barked has been laid to rest. Cory can go to his daddy's funeral now.

Gabriel made Troy a promise, and he plans to keep it. He arrives, trumpet at the ready, and announces that it's time to tell St. Peter to open the gates for Troy. He asks Troy if he's ready. This is a moment of incomparable theatrical power and majesty, intended to summon generations of African ancestors to accompany Troy Maxson through the Gates of Heaven. August Wilson's stage directions must be quoted here:

> The trumpet is without a mouthpiece. He puts the end of it into his mouth and blows with great force, like a man who has been waiting some twenty-odd years for this single moment. No sound comes out of the trumpet. He braces himself and blows again with the same result. A third time he blows. There is a weight of impossible description that falls away and leaves him bare and exposed

---

set them right down. They had become like stones and too heavy to carry. If he needed to carry something he should carry a bag of tools. He did just that. Wilson's wisest characters do not understand the futility of carrying around old sorrow, resentments, and pain. Too heavy a burden. They learn.

26. Ibid., 87–88.
27. Ibid., 88.

to a frightful realization. It is a trauma that a sane and normal mind would be unable to withstand. He begins to dance. A slow, strange dance, eerie and life-giving. A dance of atavistic signature and ritual . . . He finishes his dance and the gates of heaven stand open as wide as God's closet.[28]

Troy's redemption and journey to freedom are now fulfilled and complete. Gabriel has kept his promise. He has summoned the ancestors and called upon their customs, their traditions, and their history. They have answered and have helped to lay Troy down. Troy can now rest. There is now a sense of hope and renewal. Ghosts are banished, or at least have been duly shelved and are out of harm's way. And that is what Cory, Rose, and now Raynell need to move ahead with no shadows.

28. Ibid., 91–92.

Baltimore Center Stage 1994 Production of *Two Trains Running*,
with Anthony Chisholm. Photo by Richard Anderson.

Chapter VII

Two Trains Running

1969

De fare is cheap, an' all can go,
De rich an' poor are dere,
No second class aboard dis train,
No diffrunce in de fare.[1]

BEFUDDLED WERE MANY WHEN August Wilson's *Two Trains Running*[2] emerged in March of 1990 at the Yale Rep, and as it made its way around the residential theater circuit to open two years later on Broadway at the Walter Kerr. Its setting is the 1960s—the watershed turbulent decade that ripped apart the curtain of American innocence beginning with the November 1963 assassination of President John F. Kennedy, the vicious and painfully fractured governmental deceit that was the foreign and domestic agony of the Vietnam War, the astonishing hope of the Civil Rights revolution and its accompanying heartbreaking losses of life and dignity. In the midst of all of this came the 1968 murder and martyrdom of the Rev. Dr. Martin Luther King, Jr. and the subsequent urban riots and destruction of several major American cities, followed in just a few weeks by the shooting of the presidential candidate and second Kennedy brother, Robert. The cities continued to smolder while American blacks questioned fundamental assumptions—yet again—about the promises of freedom presumably granted to all, yet insistently denied to them. Blacks in America struggled—yet and

---

1. "Git On Board, Little Chillen," Negro Spiritual cir. seventeenth century. See Johnson and Johnson, *The Books of American Negro Spiritual*, i and 126.
2. August Wilson, *Two Trains Running*, set in 1969.

still—for a path to freedom and redemption as the rest of the country and the world watched, dumbfounded, feigning helplessness.

In August of 1968 at the Chicago Democratic Convention, American demonstrators for peace and a cease-fire in Southeast Asia were met with violence from Mayor Richard J. Daley's "peace-keeping" police forces wielding clubs and bashing skulls. A counter-weight to a non-violent civil rights revolution[3] was Malcolm X, who in 1965 had been gunned down and killed by his own colleagues in the Black Muslim religious movement. His destruction came just as he began to evolve as a moderate and humanist voice of universal justice. Stokely Carmichael, in a youthful and impatient splinter group from peacefully protesting civil rights workers, raised clenched fists and shouted "Black Power!" The phrase instilled fear of violent attack against white people. Carmichael shouted it without regard for its effect upon white sensibilities; his concern was for black empowerment. The black middle class civil rights workers became squeamish.

At the end of the decade, Republican Richard Nixon had been re-elected in 1968, and pop music legend, Marvin Gaye sang and all hummed along and asked, "What's Goin' On?"

Befuddled? Yes. *Two Trains . . .* hums along in 1969 in Memphis Lee's Hill District Pittsburgh Restaurant. It's as if the turbulent decade simply never took place. There is one mention of King[4] and several references to Malcolm X, which will be discussed in more detail. There is the issue of urban renewal that hangs over the basic story line. Audiences were at first surprised that this period piece did not more directly embrace the rich historical detail. Of course, one of the over-arching themes of this play is that no matter where on the arc of history, the Africans in America have an objective, and that is the compulsion to pose the existential questions regarding the value of black humanity in a white world—a world that is known to, without pang of conscience, deprive them of their humanity, their due, their fundamental rights, their earnings, their freedom, their right to be, their essential dignity. The struggle for the people of *Two Trains* is how do

---

3. The civil rights workers and proponents for change were non-violent. The resistance was not peaceful. It was often violent. It was characterized by terror. Bombings, beatings, lynchings, murders, fires, massacres were not at all uncommon—many committed by southern state or other government officials, or at least with their knowledge or silent assent. See, e.g., Branch, *Parting the Waters: America in the King Years 1954–63*; Branch, *Pillar of Fire: America in the King Years 1963–65*; and Branch, *At Canaan's Edge: America in the King Years 1965–68*.

4. *Two Trains*, 40.

they regain, hold onto, and succeed with what remains of their freedom. If they have now been redeemed, and if they are free, they must assume—and rightly so—that such freedom, such right to self-determination, is seen as either non-existent or in serious jeopardy. Memphis Lee discovers this. Sterling has known it. Holloway has sought out Aunt Ester and he understands the challenge. Risa takes control of her own destiny. And Hambone demands dignity.

The 1960s' freedoms held great promise. Two Acts of Congress tried to ensure that the promises of the Constitution would become fully applicable to African Americans in mid-decade.[5] Knowing just how tenuous their hold on freedom really is, they look about for which track to take for redemption. Which one of redemption's trains to take that will reap long-term rewards? Or do they want the shiny, short-term, and immediate gains to which many have often been attracted?

Two Trains is "discursive." It is a "talky" play, and may be the "least eventful" of all of the Wilson dramas. It is short on plot, yet long on ideas, and "explores big themes through small details."[6] Memphis Lee is the owner of the restaurant in which all of the action takes place. He is described as self-made and logical. He came to Pittsburgh from Jackson, Mississippi, where he bought land from some white men. The deed specified that the sale would be "null and void" if water were found on the land. Memphis found water, and the white guys voided the sale. They got the court to agree. Because Memphis fought them, they gutted his mule's stomach—thus voiding his metaphorical "40 acres and a mule," the supposed promise made to slaves by General Sherman following Emancipation.[7]

Memphis didn't forget about that. His goal is to return to Jackson to retrieve his land—to get back what he knows he deserves. First, he has to negotiate a deal with the city that wants to tear down his building. The

5. The Civil Rights Act of 1964 was passed to ensure the repeal of state and local laws that permitted segregation by race. Violations of the Act were punishable by the Federal government, for the first time in history. The Voting Rights Act of 1965 was enacted to ensure unfettered access to the voting booth for racial minorities with pre-certification rules applicable to targeted states throughout the South. The results have been revolutionary. Blacks were elected to public office all over the South, and elsewhere in the country. Its legacy is that the first black President of the United States, Barack Obama, was elected and re-elected with a majority of whites voting against him. Such was the evolved power of concentrated and focused black voting strength four decades after the 1965 Voting Rights Act.

6. Brantley, "In a Diner, Chewing the Fat and Burying the Dead."

7. Gates, Jr. and Yacovone, *The African Americans*, 127–30.

1960s urban renewal has begun, or perhaps the city wants to make way for a new highway right through the Hill district. Second, he has to get the price he wants. They have offered him a pittance, and he wants $25 thousand. He has been hardened by circumstance and brooks little nonsense, despite some nonsense going on about him all the time. He is a good man. He nourishes people when they need to be fed, he provides jobs, he tolerates their eccentricities, and he honors his history and knows its worth. Ultimately, that knowledge and appreciation sustain him.

Wolf is the typical, probably harmless, self-promoting, petty criminal, numbers runner. He takes numbers for the community locals all the time—including for Memphis on the odd occasion. Memphis's only caveat is that Wolf not take incoming calls over the restaurant telephone for fear of giving the impression that the place is some kind of "joint." Wolf has delusions of grandeur—that he's some kind of Lothario—and if he were to die soon lots of his women would weep and wail. Not true. Everybody knows it's not true. He's marginally successful at his racket, for he's not the ultimate owner, which is a white syndicate—referred to, but never seen. Wolf fancies the waitress, Risa, who is not interested. He seems to have a shallow appreciation of life, and no love at all for its complexities or shadings. For Wolf, there is no talk of true love or values or of morality.

Risa is nominally the waitress, but really manages the restaurant. She is the cook, she buys the food, she plans the menu, and she cleans. She is physically attractive and gets unwanted male attention. She appears not to be dissatisfied with being ordered about by the men who frequent the place, as if it is somehow preferable to having them regard her as some object. Her most distinguishing features are the scars on her legs. She cut her legs all over with a razor to "define herself in terms other than her genitalia."[8] Men are attracted to her, nonetheless—at least those men who have the capacity to see the scars and to comprehend their why. Risa understands more than she lets on. She was loyal to Prophet Samuel, who acquired lots of riches from poor people—including Risa. But Risa, unlike many others, knew that Prophet Samuel was no biblical prophet, but that he used some of that money to help poor people who were in trouble with legal authorities.[9]

Holloway is the character that Wilson employs to explain the supernatural—the mystical in the world of *Two Trains*. His moral compass moves him to want to right the wrongs in his world, but he lacks the ability

8. *Two Trains*, 9.
9. Ibid., 79.

to do so. Wilson writes, "Holloway is a man who all his life voiced outrage at injustice with little effect. His belief in the supernatural has enabled him to . . . pursue life with zest and vigor."[10] Holloway helps us to understand Hambone (see later discussion), but perhaps his most important function is the character he introduces. Holloway is the first to mention Aunt Ester.[11]

It is Aunt Ester who has laid the value-rich track leading from the station. Holloway knows whereof he speaks. He has been to Aunt Ester, and she showed him how to rid himself of the bad feeling he had for his own grandfather—a man who only wanted to pick cotton for white people. His grandfather loved his subservience to white oppression. Aunt Ester helped Holloway to set down that resentment against his grandfather, and to be free of it. Then Holloway serves as an emissary—to show the black oppressed a path to redemption; to Aunt Ester; to the place where she can teach how to have the souls washed.

Sterling is the character in *Two Trains* who takes a journey—a journey with Aunt Ester's help. He arrives at the restaurant having been fired from a job for lack of business. He spent some time in the penitentiary for robbing a bank. He was desperate. He was an orphan and had no money and no job. Now he can't get a job—not even at the steel mill, which should be hiring.[12] The mill says they can't hire him because he's not a member of the union, and the union wouldn't let him join because he doesn't have a job. Holloway understands the Catch-22 situation well. In slavery times when blacks worked for free and no one had to pay them, then there was more than

---

10. Ibid., 10.

11. Recall that Aunt Ester actually appears in *Gem of the Ocean*, the only play in the Cycle in which she makes an appearance. Gem was written as the penultimate play in the Cycle. *Two Trains* came 13 years before. Her debut in this play was somewhat understated, since she does not appear, but her presence in the Cycle took on far greater importance to Wilson over the years as she became the repository of wisdom, culture, history, suffering, triumph, despair, joy—all that comprised the collective experience of Africans in America—all of it. Her wisdom is sought after here, but she is clearly still in nascent development. I recall seeing this play in previews at the Kennedy Center with the late Roscoe Lee Browne in the role of Holloway. Browne went on to win a Tony nomination for his performance as Holloway. He had a wonderfully resonant baritone speaking voice that practically shook the rafters as his Holloway exhorted his colleagues to, "Go see Aunt Ester. 1839 Wylie. In the back. Go up there. A red door. Knock on that." August Wilson's characters have been knocking on that door ever since—in one way or another—to get their souls washed, to be redeemed. They are "Aunt Ester's Children." And they became her children in Memphis Lee's restaurant.

12. It is the 1960s, after all. The economy is booming, and steel is in great demand, especially in Pittsburgh.

79

enough work. Says Holloway, "They couldn't find you enough work back then. Now they got to pay you they can't find you none. If this was different time wouldn't be nobody out there in the street. They'd all be in the cotton fields."[13] Holloway sends Sterling to Aunt Ester, and Sterling invests as Aunt Ester directs. He becomes enlightened in such a way that he finds a means to put others on the right train track.[14]

Hambone is one of the familiar Wilson "spectral" characters—an oracle type—existing in his own reality. Yet Hambone, according to Wilson, plays a critical role in *Two Trains*, for his life and his death have an effect on everybody in the play.[15] The paradox is that Hambone utters only two lines: "He gonna give me my ham. I want my ham." Ten years prior to the play's opening he painted Lutz's fence. Lutz is a white man who owns a deli just across the street from Memphis's restaurant. Lutz made a promise. If Hambone did a good job he'd pay him a ham. After the job was finished, Hambone, believing that it was a good job, asked for his ham, but Lutz offered him a chicken instead. Hambone refused and has uttered those two lines ever since. He simply refuses to settle for less than what he is worth. Hambone presents his case to Lutz every single day, and repeats his complaint to everyone he meets—all the time. Holloway interprets, and articulates, the case. Hambone is no fool. He will not settle for second best. To the extent that the play is concerned with "structural racial injustice [those issues] are embodied in . . . Hambone who has been driven over the edge . . . by a deep-rooted sense of having been wronged."[16]

West is the local undertaker, and quite the successful undertaker he is. He is generally thought to have lots of money, and Holloway opines that there might be some shady dealings going on to have lined West's pockets on occasion—such as multiple use of suits or caskets. His big funeral this time is that of Prophet Samuel, a flashy "minister-type" who flaunted garish wealth with monies donated by poor people, like Risa. Many of the

13. *Two Trains*, 35. This is a fine example of one of Wilson's "blues lyrics" that abound in this, and all of his, work. It marks the end of Holloway's "Niggers ain't lazy" speech. The sound of each syllable rolls off the tongue of the actor, as if it is lifted up in an aria. The actors who are veterans of the Wilson genre all bear witness to the sheer lyricism—poetry—of the dialogue.

14. Sterling makes a return in *Radio Golf*, the final play in the Cycle. Aunt Ester's lessons learned in this play instruct the others at the end.

15. Shannon and Williams, "August Wilson Explains His Dramatic Vision: An Interview, 1991," 143.

16. Bottoms, "Two Trains Running: Blood on the Tracks," 147.

donors and followers are lined up for blocks to view his corpse, and to get close enough to rub his head for good luck. West, on Holloway's advice, had tried to see Aunt Ester, but never did. He had neither patience for the repeated attempts it would take to see a woman older than 300 years, nor tolerance for her asking people to throw their fee for her into the river. He lacks serenity.

Redemption. When Aunt Ester came to be she spoke to Wilson as an African woman whose first feeling on this foreign soil was that of discomfort, for "there were no spirits in the trees."[17] She then becomes at first one of the means of finding identity, a central spirit for knowing that essence of the people who inhabit the Wilson world. She evolves in the artist's imagination to call on her children—the survivors of slavery's mayhem, its legacy, and their descendants—to make that essential voyage to discovery to know self and to free self of the burden of the past. Not to forget the past—no, never that—but to liberate self of the past's heaviness, to set down those weighty stones of resentments, prejudices, anger, and to step onto a Higher Ground, a new plateau. Soul washed and fully redeemed. She uses all of the tools of the culture, and Wilson explores the creative tension between what is African in spirit in his characters and what they have adapted as their Christianity. The two spiritual belief systems creatively coexist in powerful tension in Aunt Ester, as she counsels her Citizen Barlow on the wisdom of Jesus Christ in *Gem*, while preparing him to get his soul washed in the City of Bones—a mythical place at the bottom of the Atlantic Ocean. She embodies that coexistence as it has inhabited African Americans for generations. Wilson delivers wonderfully in that blues/spiritual and sacred/secular territory in every play in the Cycle—theologically, culturally, historically—and in the dialogue. For Wilson, Aunt Ester opened up a literary and spiritual landscape of plenteous opportunity. And for her children in *Two Trains*, she lays before them in Holloway's voice the one and only track of true value and true meaning.

If Memphis Lee gets the right price for his restaurant, he will not only redeem his Mississippi land, but he will also open a nice place at the bottom of the Hill—not on a side street, but on Centre Avenue.

West is the bearer of the dead, all of the dead who lived on the surface of life—Begaboo, who was only a boy, and Patchneck Red, who was a gambler and on whose grave people come to drink, party, and gamble as

---

17. October 18, 2012 Conversation with Todd Kreidler, August Wilson Dramaturge, 1999–2006.

if on the neon-drenched Las Vegas strip. West has only money, and since his wife's death money "overshadows the other possibilities in his life."[18] He grieved for his dead wife and wanted to know if she was in heaven. He needed to be free of grief and worry and concern. He went to see Aunt Ester. Yet his money—albeit a relative pittance—was so important that when she told him to throw the requisite $20 in the river, he thought she was too old and had lost her mind. He would never do such a crazy thing as throw money away. He didn't understand that in order to gain wisdom, you had to *do* something. Holloway, the wise one tells him (to no avail), "You don't want to do nothing for yourself. You want somebody else to it for you. Aunt Ester don't work that way. She say you got to pull your share of the load. But you didn't want to do that. That's why you don't know. And it didn't cost you but twenty dollars."[19]

Wilson says that redemption requires independent action, not reliance on anybody else. Was this his answer, or his question, from the turbulent 60s from which much of the black population finds itself still stuck, mired in a maelstrom of poor schools—walking out of them undereducated, barely literate, yet infuriatingly self-satisfied? Is this what the Wilson challenge is to the community to find the ways of freedom through the wisdom of Aunt Ester? Pick up that ball and run with it?

West, lover of all things material, makes several unacceptably low offers to Memphis for the building, but West does not understand that Memphis has been to see Aunt Ester, and that Memphis now trusts his own understanding of how he must proceed with the negotiations with the white people. And it is Aunt Ester's fortification that emboldens him to go after that amount that exceeds his expectations by ten thousand dollars. And he gets it. He has tapped into his reserve of pride, his history, his humanity, and his muscle. He prevailed.

Sterling finds his way to Aunt Ester, who in her own way does nothing to deter him from his romantic intentions toward Risa. He goes to Risa in the restaurant, woos her, dances with her, sings to her the blues: "I got everything, Set your poor heart at ease, I got everything for you, woman."[20] She falls for him (who wouldn't, after that song?), for he sees her legs and understands her, he sees *her.*

18. *Two Trains*, 35.

19. Ibid., 70.

20. Ibid., 89.

In a curtsey to the times, Wilson ponders the choice: Malcolm X, in whose memory a birthday rally is to held,[21] or Prophet Samuel, who Risa points out, was sent by God to help colored people get justice? Yet, neither is the right track to redemption. Not even Hambone can be convinced. One day in the restaurant, Sterling tries to get Hambone to chant something other the demand for the ham. "Black is beautiful! . . . United we stand! . . . Malcolm lives!"[22] Hambone will have none of it. He knows what his demand is, and he knows how he has been cheated. All the slogans in the world are no substitute for standing up and facing down the power that refuses to make good on what he deserves, what he has earned, and what is due. He is unwilling to just accept whatever the white world throws at him.

One day Hambone does not show up. He's been found dead, just lying across his bed. Everyone except West is saddened by Hambone's death. Well, perhaps West is sad, given that he complains about the cost of a government-subsidized burial, which Hambone must have, and how much he's losing on the deal. This is when Aunt Ester's rejection of materialism comes into focus. Memphis, Sterling, and Holloway have received her wisdom, and her ministry, unlike that of Prophet Samuel, is not about the accumulation of money, but on its unimportance—a value system, wisdom, and tradition. This is about rejection of this false and tinny materialism.

Shocked at the news of his death, Memphis mourns Hambone, and he quotes Aunt Ester in memory of Hambone and on behalf of everyone who has ever dropped the ball and gone back to pick it up, as Hambone did every day. Aunt Ester says:

> "If you drop the ball, you got to go back and pick it up. Ain't no need in keeping running, cause if you get to the end zone, it ain't gonna be a touchdown." She didn't say it in them words, but that's what she meant. Told me . . . "You got to go back and pick up the ball."[23]

Sterling, having been redeemed, breaks into Lutz's store, takes a ham, drops it on the restaurant counter in front of West, and, in the final words of the play, tells West that the ham is for Hambone's casket. He redeems Hambone. He is bleeding from his face and his hands. He has shed the requisite

21. Memphis Lee is quick to remind everyone that dead men can't have birthdays. *Two Trains*, 39. Wilson explores what dead men can no longer enjoy in *King Hedley II* when Elmore and King discuss what it means to have killed another man.

22. *Two Trains*, 59–60.

23. Ibid., 98.

blood in this final act of redemption. You cannot wait for it. You must take it. Pick up the ball. Pull your share of the load. The simple demand will never do. This is Sterling's profound and powerful witness—the willingness to bleed—to shed blood to be redeemed.

And thus it is Aunt Ester. It is not Malcolm, nor Prophet Samuel. The train to take has value. It has depth. It has richness and lore and culture and history and myth and spirit and wonder. It has truth.

Baltimore Center Stage 1999 Production of *Jitney*, with Paul Butler and Keith Randolph Smith. Photo by Richard Anderson.

CHAPTER VIII

Paying Redemption's Dues

Jitney

1977

AUGUST WILSON WROTE THE earliest version of *Jitney*[1] in 1979, long before he conceived of the idea of the Century Cycle. It is set in Pittsburgh in 1977. He submitted it to the Eugene O'Neill Theater Center National Playwright's Conference, and it was rejected. He rewrote it, and it was rejected again. His third submission garnered an acceptance and a $2,500 Jerome Fellowship. It received a staged reading at the Penumbra Theater in St. Paul, Minnesota, in 1981, where it played to standing room only audiences. It was the first time many in the audience had been to the theater in their lives. The wonder was that people like them were on the stage, and it was a unique experience. Wilson understood that he had the ability to reach these audiences. Yet it was not until *Ma Rainey*[2] that he was to become known.

People love August Wilson's *Jitney*. This is a statement of fact. Every theater, every director, every cast member has the same experience. People love it. It comes as close to the Saturday afternoon black male barber shop cross talk as any other play in existence. It's as if, as Ishmael Reed wrote in the foreword to the TCG edition of the play, Wilson had recorded conversations and later sat to listen over and over to capture the cadences, the rhythms, the back and forth, the philosophies, the poetry, the lyricism, and the joy whenever black men gather. As Reed points out, Wilson has them banter, for example, about the beauty of Sarah Vaughan versus Lena Horne.

1. August Wilson, *Jitney*, set in 1977.
2. *Ma Rainey's Black Bottom*, 1984.

It's about dreams, but it's also that beauty by which Wilson brings the blues to the page, that is then intoned by the actor's voice. Reed compares him to writers such as Langston Hughes and Ernest J. Gaines. I would also add Gwendolyn Brooks and Rita Dove. In the end, as one character says, it all comes down to what will get you killed: money and women. And that's the blues.[3]

The substantially revised *Jitney* began its journey to New York with a premiere at the Pittsburgh Public Theater in 1996, and opened at the Second Stage Theatre in 2000. And even after its many revisions and its popularity, it still reveals an early and developing August Wilson in that it is not characterized by many (it has *some* beauties) of the long, poetic, and lyrical soliloquies for which his later classics became known. Nor does it contain the later characteristic mysticism, theology, and layers of consciousness and history that require the attention and acute awareness of his audiences. Yet its remarkably short length permits a sharpened focus on the essential father–son struggle that makes it arguably his most accessible and straightforward play in the Cycle.

> . . . *But I trust in Your faithfulness,*
> *my heart will exult in Your deliverance.*
> *I will sing to the Lord,*
> *For He has been good to me.*[4]

Jitney is about five men who drive gypsy cabs in the black Hill district of Pittsburgh. The realities of urban economic and racial segregation had effects that were (and are) legion, and that often meant that white cabs would not pick up black passengers nor deliver them to black neighborhoods. It was not at all uncommon that retired or second-job men would drive their own "gypsy" cars to meet the need. In some cities the places from which the businesses operated were called jitney stations. They typically had a pay phone, the number on which customers could call, and a set of rules about the rotation of jobs, the cleanliness of the cars and driver comportment. In Wilson's *Jitney*, the station from which the five men work is owned and operated by Becker. And he does, in fact, have rules: no overcharging; keep the car clean; no drinking (an especially difficult challenge for Fielding, an alcoholic); be courteous; and replace and clean tools.

---

3. See the foreword by Ishmael Reed, *Jitney*, vii–xvi.
4. Psalm 13:6 (JPS).

Becker is retired from the lumber mill. He is a community pillar—an established fact that becomes a source of tension between Becker and his son Booster. Booster is Becker's only child, a first-class intellect and brilliant scholar with limitless potential who was falsely accused of raping a white girl. Her father was a big oil company executive. Instead of waiting to have the truth adduced at trial—that the sex was consensual—Booster shot the girl dead at point blank range, and was sentenced to death. Grief overwhelmed his mother, who died shortly after that. The death sentence was then commuted to life. The major father–son confrontation follows Booster's unconditional release from prison. He and his father see each other and speak for the first time in 22 years. Becker never appeared at his trial, nor did he visit his son in prison. He abandoned his son. Booster seeks reconciliation—forgiveness. He shares his story of redemption. It's too late for Becker.

Turnbo, a retiree, is a nosy busybody of the worst sort. His persistent meddling in everybody's personal business can be amusing, but it also inflicts considerable damage and wounds egos. Doub is a Korean War veteran, a solid guy with sound judgment. He serves as Wilson's dramatic device to bring everybody and the action back on an even keel. Youngblood[5] is the youngest of the men and just back from the fighting jungles of Vietnam. He has a two year-old son and a girlfriend for whom he has just purchased a house with which he will surprise her. She (Rena) is, of course, happy about the house, but most unpleasantly shocked about the very idea of surprising her with . . . a house that they have not chosen together. Men. Fielding, as mentioned, is an alcoholic for whom Becker has lost patience and wants gone. But in a continuing and consistent theme (excepting his own son), Becker forgives (enables) him, and keeps him on.[6]

Wilson places these men in this hardscrabble, storefront commercial space, swapping stories in his lyrical and bluesy manner. The very essence—the core—of *Jitney* is responsibility. These five, colorful black men have taken upon themselves the duty—the responsibility—to see that their lives and the lives of the people they love are well-cared for. They pay money to Becker to be there—to drive to pick up the passengers; they carry their

5. The name, "Youngblood," was what an old guy in the Hill district called Wilson as he coached him to stop carrying around ten-gallon buckets to fill, but to carry cups instead. We hear this in "How I Learned What I Learned."

6. Two others: Shealy is a numbers runner who is in and out of the scenes. He has some gorgeous blues soliloquies. Philmore is a hotel doorman, a frequent station visitor and jitney passenger.

share of the load of life. They make jobs out of nothing. "[Jitney] was an attempt to show what the community was like at the time. The important thing was for me to show these five guys working and creating something out of nothing."[7]

Aunt Ester was not a part of August Wilson's consciousness at this time, yet this statement becomes a building block of the very foundation that would become her wisdom. You must pull your share of the load, take responsibility, and if you drop the ball, go back and pick it up, otherwise it won't be a touchdown. That is the only way to find redemption, and that is to get up and do something about it.[8] Then you will have all that you need, and you will know how God has been faithful to you, and whatever else you might need to be free. You will then be able to rejoice and be glad.

The large factual issue in *Jitney* is that the city, engaged in urban renewal, has announced plans to tear down the building that holds the jitney station. The five men, after a somewhat tortured and worried day or so, finally agree that they will stay put and not move unless and until the city makes a move to board up the building. Even then they will pool their resources to fight. It is an act of defiance, which bespeaks empowerment and faith in God's abiding love. The God who redeemed them to arrive at the place of being able to make something from nothing will see them through.

It is as if they were making quilts from patches of their lives—patches that alone may have no intrinsic value at all—but put together, serve as powerful testimony to God's unchanging faithfulness and love, and that serve to protect and to save them from destruction.

Becker and Booster. Becker's sure-footed manner and no-nonsense style around his jitney station betray none of the internal misery and bitterness he holds from the tragedy of his son's fall. The play takes a sudden turn, and a great Becker could wear on his face this lament:

> *How long, O Lord; will You ignore me forever?*
> *How long will You hide Your face from me?*
> *How long will I have cares on my mind,*
> *grief in my heart all day?*[9]

Wilson hangs the cloud of the great meeting between father and son, which will (as in *Fences* between Troy and Cory) contain a great theological

---

7. Shannon and Williams, "August Wilson Explains his Dramatic Vision," 126.

8. See *Two Trains*, Act 2, Scene 5.

9. Psalm 13:1–3 (JPS).

debate about the nature of redemption, forgiveness, and reconciliation. The problem here is that we have no preparation for it. There is some mention of Booster by the gossip, Turnbo, in the first Act, but Becker carries no hint of sorrow and bespeaks no measure of his personal alienation from God—that God has turned away from him. Such a fundamental absence of faith is not merely incidental among black men of that day (or any day for that matter), it is profoundly remarkable. And such alienation would have been at least hinted at much earlier in the narrative.

To achieve his redemption, Becker will die, just as a similarly tortured soul, Troy Maxson, had to die. Fathers and sons who are deeply and intractably estranged are not permitted—in the Cycle—to reconcile before the father's death. It is a tragic assessment and perhaps reflects the nature of Wilson's undocumented relationship with his own father, who apparently abandoned his family.

Becker, having just discovered the city's plans for the neighborhood, has rational and sensible Doub work through some options given the latest developments. In moments, the mood shifts as Becker hears the news of Booster's imminent release from prison. Becker then tells all about reaching for God, for answers, and finding nothing there. He says to Doub:

> I used to question God about everything. Why he hardened Pharaoh's heart? Why he let Jacob steal his brother's birthright? After Coreen[10] died I told myself I wasn't gonna ask no more questions. Cause the answers didn't matter. They didn't matter right then. I thought that would change but it never did. It still don't matter after all these years. It don't look like it's never gonna matter. I'm tired of waiting for God to decide whether he want to hold my hand . . .[11]

Becker gets his chance to find out just how much God is there for him when Booster comes, having fully paid for, bought back his identity and his dignity, and wants to scoop up his father with him in one glorious gust of redemptive love and forgiveness. The paradox is that Becker feels that God, the Father, abandoned him, and it is Becker, the father, who in turn abandoned his own son. Perhaps the way back to the fold of faith is through the

10. His wife, Booster's mother, who died from grief after Booster was sentenced to death.

11. *Jitney*, 26. This dirge is resonant in substance to Levee's rage in *Ma Rainey*. The same question is asked of God, demanding an answer, "Where the hell were you when I needed you?"

return into the arms of his child, who loves and forgives him. But the shock of it all is too much for Becker to handle, as his departing words to his son are, "You ain't nothing to me, boy. You just another nigger on the street."[12]

Booster and Becker's confrontation reopens all of the old and ghastly wounds—all the blood let out onto the floor and spurted all over them with accusations and reprisals. A lot needed to be said—a mother and wife they both loved, each at fault, the painful truths had to be spoken. They could be held no more. The moment, however, is Booster's. He knows all too well the horror, the humiliation and hell that came from the gruesome murder and that stupid error in judgment that was his, and his, alone. But he paid. And he paid the price—in full. He turned down parole so that he would have no one to answer to. He stands before his father a free man—a redeemed man—a whole man.

Becker asks why—why he didn't wait for the truth of the lie at trial. That he did not rape that white girl. That she lied. Booster has the answer, and it's the answer that Becker does not want to hear. Booster recalls the excruciating pain in boyhood of seeing the bigness of his father—a Big man in black Pittsburgh, this Pillar of the Community, reduced to a boy as his white landlord knocked him on his ass for being late with the household rent. Booster swore to himself that he would redeem his father's (and his own) honor whenever he had the opportunity. To kill that lying white girl was that redemptive opportunity, and that warrior in him would not countenance white supremacy or oppression.[13] He said that he knew that this was a way that his father could not deal with the world. Becker had responsibilities that his son did not have.

Becker would have none of it. He snorted at the very idea that his son killed a woman because a white man knocked down his dad so that the family would not be set out into the street in the middle of winter without a roof over their heads. He told Booster that he killed his mother when she heard the death sentence for her son. Booster, on the other hand, shot back that Becker needed to respond to the white landlord in the way that he needed to. Booster had no such limitations. He needed to be able to

---

12. Ibid., 46.

13. The Wilson warriors who commit serious mistakes and crimes, yet they fight to preserve honor and integrity—respect and principles—as discussed on page 59 of "How I Learned What I Learned." Booster, with this soliloquy, mistaken, but noble, places himself among the other Warriors in the Cycle: Solly Two Kings in *Gem*; Herald Loomis in *Joe Turner*; Levee in *Ma Rainey*; Willie Boy in *Piano Lesson*; Floyd Barton in *Seven Guitars*; Troy in *Fences*; Sterling in *Two Trains* and *Radio Golf*; and King in *King Hedley*.

live with himself. He did it for himself, it was a mistake, it didn't add up. Now he's paid for it. As for his mother, he tells his dad that she needed her husband's support in the courtroom—that she was left to shoulder the grief alone.

There is too much hurt and pain between them. Booster has had the time—and the desire—to free himself and to be redeemed. Becker dismisses him as he himself believes that God has dismissed him.

Becker dies the next day in a freak accident at his part-time job at the lumber mill. There was no time for lifetime reconciliation. He has been redeemed in death. Booster rises and takes over the management of the jitney station. It is his final act of forgiveness and acceptance of responsibility for the damage his crime caused his family. He rescues what is left and makes something out of nothing—as his father had done for years. He is redeemed.

Arena Stage 2015 Production of King Hedley II, with Jessica Frances Dukes, Kenyatta Rogers, Bowman Wright, E. Faye Butler, Michael Anthony Williams, and Andre DeShields. C. Stanley Photography.

CHAPTER IX

Danger—All About Them—Danger

King Hedley II

1985

EVERYWHERE AND AT EVERY opportunity a weapon of destruction appears. Without warning, without pause or thought or pang of conscience of portentous and imminent lethality, a gun or rifle will be brandished proudly and passed around and admired like a new toy or a wristwatch. It would not be unlike the extended family reaction back in the days of more deeply-rooted and valued pride, the way a newly-minted academic degree or certificate would evoke the smiles and spontaneous bursts of applause, with hugs, kisses, pinches on the cheeks, and pats on the back at the family cook out. Black people in America assumed then that they inhabited a world that, at a minimum, acknowledged its identity and humanity.

August Wilson's view of 1985 obliterates that assumption. The audiences are held in their seats as if by some powerful force determined to rip down the veil of illusion that leaves them staring and unblinking at awful truths of a people at the edge of the abyss. Relief comes only by asking, "What happened?" And the question brings that scintilla of hope; for the answer is that miracle of resilience and survival of the displaced people of the African diaspora.

The characters in *King Hedley II*[1] inhabit a 1985 Hill District that is not merely bleak—that the audience would settle for about halfway through the first act—but it is a small world inexorably headed for self-destruction. The

---

1. August Wilson, *King Hedley II*, set in 1985.

people have lost their love of the past; they have lost their identities; they have lost their songs; and, inexplicably, the audience feels complicit.[2]

We know that humankind over all time has not changed, and absent some fundamental cataclysmic alteration in the nature of creation, humankind will not change. All of our ancient drawings and texts, and ancient dramas, provide ample attestation to this truth. The same imperatives that have moved humans for millennia still move us today—love, jealousy, betrayal, lust, power, greed, loss, grief, madness. Humans have always had the means to wipe one another from the face of the earth—to battle until the last one stands, and before the next to the last hits the ground to cast the last stone, leaving both to return to the dust. Such has never happened, and thus we can be reasonably assured that it will not. That is the good news. The bad news is our history, and that we have the capacity and the will to exact untold horrors upon one another as we approach the brink of annihilation. That brink is the point to which August Wilson takes the African in America in his 1985 Pittsburgh Hill District.

But he who listens to me will dwell in safety,

Untroubled by the terror of misfortune.[3]

Hedley II is a play of epic ambition and scope. It begins with a Shakespearean-style prologue intoned by the prescient, observant, keeper of the history, the 65-year-old Stool Pigeon.[4] His prologue is spoken on a calm, clear, and starry night that "belies the approaching tempest."[5] His message is that things are not the way they were. People are not listening to the wisdom of their ancestors, as they have been doing in all of the prior plays of the Cycle—or at least have been coming to that point of knowledge

---

2. Complicit perhaps because the tragic circumstances of the 1980s Hill district are markedly similar to most of urban America of the same era—and the legacy still haunts us. Few African Americans could look upon such devastation and not ask what he/she could have done to avert the crisis, to save one person, to stop the senseless shooting, the violence, to see to the education of one child at-risk. Guilt? Art forces us to see ourselves as true and to confront the Truth. Sometimes it "ain't pretty." The *King Hedley* experience was/is such a time.

3. Proverbs 1:33 (JPS).

4. Stool Pigeon is Canewell from *Seven Guitars*. When Hedley appears with Floyd's cash after Floyd's burial, Canewell knows that Hedley is Floyd's murderer, and tells the police. Ruby thus began calling him Stool Pigeon, and the name stuck. He prefers to be called, as he says in this play, "Truthsayer."

5. *Hedley*, 7.

by reaching a redemptive stage, often a point of epiphany. Stool Pigeon is seemingly spent of all hope:

> Everything done got broke up . . . Look like it's gonna be broke up some more before it get whole again. If it ever do . . . .The people don't know but God gonna tell it . . . .The people . . . They got lost. They don't even know the story of how they got from tit to tat. Aunt Ester know. But the path to her house is all grown over with weeds, you can't hardly find the door no more . . . .The people need to know the story. See how they fit into it. See what part they play. [God] say, "Let him who have wisdom understand." Aunt Ester got the wisdom. She three hundred sixty-six years old. She got the Book of Life.[6]

And thus, through Stool Pigeon, the Truthsayer, August Wilson re-establishes his basic truth—that which he has demonstrated throughout the prior eight plays of the Cycle—that the key to redemption for the African in America, to wholeness, to freedom, is to know the history and to call upon it, as Berniece does at long last when she sits down at that piano in *The Piano Lesson*. And to know that history—how they got from "tit to tat"—is to know their identity. Who you are.[7] Then there is the need to know the ancestral wisdom, culture, and traditions. The faith in the Christianity of the enslavers alone was never enough; in fact, for some it was actively harmful, for it was designed for further subjugation. Africans in America required more and designed a God—a Christian God that was also an active and interrupting God of liberation, a God that combined the spirits of the tribal heritages and the more distant God of the enslaver. The God of the African in America was present in spirit and inhabited an immediate and often an inanimate world. Aunt Ester embodied that amalgam of spirituality and belief, and she embodied the ancestral history, wisdom, culture, practices, joys, sorrows, and beliefs.

Stool Pigeon's prologue puts us on notice that Aunt Ester's children are in real danger. No longer do they seek her guidance, nor her wisdom, for it's been so long since anyone has been to see her that the path to her home is now overgrown with weeds. When a people stop seeking the wisdom of the ancestors, then there is trouble, indeed. Wilson writes this prologue to warn us that Aunt Ester's children are not merely adrift; they are

---

6. Ibid., 7–8.

7. See, Deuteronomy 6:10–12 (JPS) " . . . do not forget the Lord who freed you . . . "

sinking. They are losing their very identity—on the verge of being wiped out—obliterated.

Stool Pigeon, who hoards every single newspaper from every single day, such that he can barely walk into his own house ("what's in them newspapers is important; we have to know how we got from tit to tat"), understands the enormous price of destruction of "self."

But there is a resurrection. There is light to pierce the gloom. Again in a tense coexistence of Christian and African traditions—in the ancient Yoruban tradition of the sacrifice of one to save the lives of many[8]—the blood of one is shed to redeem the lives of those he loves. Stool Pigeon can end this play on the Hill in Hope and Joy in the wake of a Resurrection.[9]

Despite its challenges for audiences (Hedley is not one of Wilson's most popular plays, and because of its grit perhaps never will be), it contains some of the most beautiful speeches Wilson wrote for the Cycle. Every time Ruby opens her mouth for an extended time, she sings the blues, and the conversations between and among the male characters about their relationships with God before and after taking the life of another human, or what it means to murder someone, to take another life, are profound and worthy of revisits to any *Hedley* production. I have often felt that Elmore was an unfinished character in this play—that his shifts in points of view are unaccounted for.[10] I still think so. Yet Wilson has written beautifully for him. He'll remain unfinished; the running time on the play is long enough.

Who are they? King has a massive and defining scar on his face running from forehead to the bottom of his chin. Like his supposed father, King Hedley I, he lives by his own set of standards and moral code. And similar to several other Wilson men, he lives in his own reality, which in his case can easily be regarded as slightly irrational and at times explosive with anger. Some man named Pernell cut King's face with a razor for a minor violation of the street code. In an act of revenge, King shot Pernell several times to kill him. That was a few days later. This all made perfect sense to King, as he reasoned that if a black man entered a white man's house and

---

8. Mbiti, *Introduction to African Religion*, 63.

9. *Hedley*, 109–10.

10. At one point he instructs Stool Pigeon that God is not a factor in his life, or in his life's choices. Later in dialogue with King, Elmore speaks mournfully of what murder does to a man's relationship with God. Moreover, he hints that he must disclose the great truth of the play to King, in order to set things right with God—hinting that he is *in extremis*. Such inconsistencies in Elmore are undeveloped. But the play—running time of 2 hours and 45 minutes—is almost too long.

stole a TV, and the white man shot him, the white people would say that the black man had it coming to him. But Pernell cut his face, and he shot him. Well, cutting a man's face was infinitely worse than stealing a TV. Why should King be punished? Why isn't this act of killing justifiable, as well?[11] King spent seven year in prison for that crime.

King gives voice to the American black man's fury and frustrations at living as a discounted being in a white world. He takes his receipt to a store where he had some pictures developed of and for his wife, Tonya. The pictures weren't there; they couldn't be found. King didn't understand because he had the receipt. The store manager told him that the receipt didn't count, since the whole system is based on telephone numbers. King was confused and livid because he knew that this was yet another white-man scheme to deny a black man a chance to carry out a simple and insignificant transaction—just because he could, and for no other reason. When white people deal with black people, the rules suddenly change. The receipt system had always worked until he needed it, and now that he needs it—new rules. Here August Wilson taps into a familiar source of black rage; not the example, the issue—moving the ball just as you are about to kick it. You fall on your ass.

King's relationship with his mother Ruby is strained. She left him to be raised by her aunt, Louise.[12] As King sees it, Ruby abandoned him and he has no time or respect for her. He makes that clear. He glorifies his father's legacy, however, and exhibits many of his eccentricities.

King has a friend named Mister, with whom he is a partner in crime—store robberies, fraudulent appliance sales to neighbors, gambling, gun sales. Guns appear as if they are bars of candy. King also has a wife, Tonya, who in turn has a daughter Natasha, by another man. Natasha is in her early teens, and she, too, is adrift in a world of misplaced values. Like her mother before her, Natasha is having sex with too many men at too young an age. Tonya is pregnant with King's child and is most unhappy about it.

King's one act of faith and hope in the future over which he has control is that he has planted flower seeds, although Ruby thinks it is wasted in bad dirt—perhaps a metaphor for Tonya's dilemma. Ruby's hopelessness

11. Ibid., 59.

12. This is the Louise from *Seven Guitars*, who refers to her "fast behind" niece, Ruby, from Alabama. Ruby had to come to Pittsburgh to escape "man trouble." She was pregnant with Leroy's son, Hedley. Another man, Elmore, in a jealous rage over Ruby, killed Leroy. Ruby had to get out of town, and showed up on Louise's doorstep—with her "fast behind." Indeed.

does not deter King, even as he protects his flowerbed with barbed wire. Ruby would surely know the futility of investing in "bad dirt." It has defined her life—bad choices in men—bad choices with respect to her son. It is an obvious metaphor.

Tonya grieves over regret. She, too, has made bad choices and they have come back to visit her in her daughter. Her own pregnancy provides an opportunity to look over her life, and what she sees is not at all a place into which she wants to bring new life. It's images of terror—weapons, crime, razors, murder, grief, and God's absence while boys pretending to be men try to take His place. There is history's destruction, children killing children, undertakers' telephone lines with busy signals, while mothers' hot dinners for their boys languish on kitchen tables until cold because their sons won't be home; their young bodies are stiffening in the morgue waiting to be identified. And then, she can't justify having a baby who will be younger than her grandchild.[13] And in the hands of the right artist this speech could soar as a blues ballad spoken in a voice that would have the audience begging for more. As it is, most actors deliver it over-wrought and angry. Understood. But it is also a deep and soulful wail of woe. And for just once—just once—I would love to find a production that would take the risk of slowing it down to its mournful depth. This is August Wilson's blues at its best, and it should be delivered that way. Consider a slow delivery of this:

> I ain't raising no kid to have somebody shoot him. To have his friends shoot him. To have the police shoot him. Why I want to bring another life into this world that don't respect life? I don't want to raise no more babies when you got to fight to keep them alive. You take little Buddy Will's mother up on Bryn Mawr Road. What she got? A heartache that don't never go away. She up there now sitting down in her living room. She got to sit down 'cause she can't stand up. She sitting down trying to figure it out. Trying to figure out what happened. One minute her house is full of life. The next minute it's full of death. She was waiting for him to come home and they bring her a corpse.[14]

13. Much of this, and more, is set forth in Tonya's great speech that has become a classic for the character and in the Cycle. Tonya was given greatest life by a then (2001) relatively unknown Viola Davis when the play opened at Washington's Kennedy Center, its last stop prior to New York. I saw her deliver that speech, and I said, "That will get her a Tony." It did. Ibid., 40–42.

14. Ibid., 41.

The raw power of the speech is only enhanced by a slower cadence and delivery. That is when the nature of the blues and the poetry comes out in full flower and force. The notions of sitting down in grief, and standing up in grief and not finding comfort or solace in either rips us apart—nothing helps.

Tonya also loses faith in her future with King. Each time she sees him with Mister, always there is a new pistol, or a fresh wad of cash, and she knows that there has been, or that there will be, a new crime committed. She wants no part of a future with King in prison. We also discover that when she was pregnant with Natasha she went to see Aunt Ester, because she thought that Aunt Ester was whom she should see to get an abortion. She found out just the opposite. Aunt Ester was where she would find out how to cope with life—to pick up her share of the load—to take responsibility. She found herself there. She found the pieces of herself and became whole. Aunt Ester laid her hand upon her, and Tonya found peace. She was refreshed—redeemed. There she found her song. Now, she would need that again.

But the path to Aunt Ester's is overgrown. 1839 Wylie—the Sanctuary, the Peaceful Place—is no longer accessible. People have stopped seeking her wisdom. They have separated themselves from their history, and what has grounded them. Stool Pigeon comes with the news that Aunt Ester, who was never to die, has died. She has died of grief. She died with her hand stuck to her head as if to say, "What has happened to my children, Lord? Oh my God, what shall I do? Have you forsaken us?" Three hundred sixty-six years old. The separation from her children who needed her, but who had forgotten—or neglected—to see her, killed her. Their lives have been tragic, and that has grieved her to death. The coroner has taken her body. He wants to know what happened to make her live so long. Her people want to know what happened to make her die so soon.

At the moment of her death, lights went out all over town. The light of the world has gone. And in an ancient African tradition the people will stand and keep vigil until the body is buried. This woman of strength and embodiment and wisdom has survived the middle passage, the terrors of slavery, the first joys of freedom, the humiliations and the horrors of Jim Crow, and now this. Such a stunning statement of devastation and despair about a people unmoored and valueless represented in her demise. But it is Stool Pigeon who takes her dead cat, buries it with the belief that if the blood of an animal or human is sacrificed and spilled on that grave, there will be a resurrection of spirit and hope, and there will be redemption and salvation made possible for many.

Elmore is a man in his 60s. He has known Ruby for a long time. They have been periodic lovers, the type who have never really been able to work it out, but have always had that chemistry. It's that kind of powerful chemistry that's best remembered from long ago and far away. It's irresistible trouble.[15] Elmore turns up after many years, and more than a few of those years were spent in prison for having murdered Ruby's lover, Leroy Slater, in a jealous rage back in Birmingham. And when he murders Leroy, he knows that Ruby is pregnant with Leroy's child. When Ruby arrives in Pittsburgh, early in her pregnancy and not showing it, she makes love to Hedley and leads him and everyone else to believe that the son, King, to whom she gives birth, is Hedley's child. Only Elmore knows the truth.

He has come to Pittsburgh for his brand of small-time hustle, of course. But he has also come to accomplish two more serious objectives: first, to stake what he believes is his rightful claim to Ruby's love; and second, to tell King the truth about his father—that Leroy is his real father, and not Hedley, and that he, Elmore, murdered him. Ruby is delighted at the prospect of love, but terrified that the secret she wanted to carry to her grave might be revealed. To her, it is just another form of destruction, danger, a shooting, a smashing of a badly concocted tale, the foundation of which could never withstand the mayhem all around her.

After *Seven Guitars*, Ruby became a lounge singer and performed in clubs all around the country. The price she's paid is King's resentment in not having his mother present in his life. He even wants her to leave, and repeatedly asks her to go now that Louise has died.[16] And although Ruby, like Tonya, has fears and misgivings about the men around her going back to prison, unlike Tonya Ruby is attracted to the elements of danger about her. She seems to thrive on being in the midst of bad men. She is intrigued—not fearful—when Mister takes his new-just-purchased-from-Elmore silver and mother-of-pearl derringer out of his pocket. She holds it, cocks it for shooting, and boasts when Mister gives her the derringer that, "I wanna see somebody mess with me now."[17] She is not at all put off by these weapons. She has a violent streak. In fact, she can get closer to the violence, if need be—by using her hand. She tells a story about how a man

15. See note 241.

16. *Hedley*, 12.

17. Ibid., 87. I have seen this scene played with an erotic caress of the pistol.

gave her unwanted attention and she broke a bottle on the side of his car, cutting her hand in the process, then putting the jagged glass to his throat, and threatening to shove it in.

> Blood was running all down my hand and everywhere. I told him to lick it. I told him I wanted him to taste my blood 'cause if he didn't move his hand from under my dress I was gonna taste his. I rubbed my hand all over his face. There was blood everywhere. My hand looked like it wasn't gonna stop bleeding. He moved his hand and I got out of the car. I found out later I was on my period and I got mad. I told myself I wished I had cut him 'cause there wasn't nobody's blood in the car but mine.[18]

Ruby sings the blues here—classic—raw with a hint of the humor in the unexpected that characterizes a blues lyric. This is typical of the Ruby speeches in *Hedley*. The concept of shedding blood for a purpose, here to protect her honor, runs throughout the play, as it does in the Cycle. Shedding blood as a sacrifice to be redeemed, e.g., Herald Loomis in *Joe Turner*, as he slashes himself in baptism, "I can bleed for myself"; or the reference to Mama Ola in *The Piano Lesson*, rubbing the wood of the piano until she bled, and her blood was mixed in with the wood.

God?

What does August Wilson convey about a murderous human being's relationship with God in King Hedley II, a world where God, and the person who is arguably God's emissary to the people—Aunt Ester—have gone and abandoned it? That emissary has died of grief over the ways of her people who have strayed from her values, her traditions, her core beliefs. Ruby robs her own child of his true identity, his self, his song, then does what God wants no mother to do. She abandons him, and in the end she takes his life.

Then Wilson crafts a series of transcendent dialogues between Elmore and King about their self-revelatory relationships with God, and what happens to that after murdering another human—another man. A small sample:

> Elmore: See, when you pulled that trigger you done something....
> you done been God. Death is something he do. God decide when

18. Ibid., 84.

somebody ready. Not you. He decide when he want somebody. God don't like that, you thinking you him. He cut you loose.

King: Anybody kill somebody is living without God. You ain't even got no right to pray. When Mama Louise died . . . [s]he told me she was gonna leave me in the hands of God. She didn't know that I had already messed that up.

Elmore: Anybody kill somebody is on their own.[19]

The profoundly tragic sadness of this dialogue is rooted in their belief that God is absent from them, and conversely that their acts of murder have taken them beyond—outside—the ambit of God's love and mercy. It is where they are in the 1985 world of the Hill district. Elmore and King see a world of utter despair, a life devoid of hope. Just darkness. It is the classic definition of Hell—alienation from God. They have come to believe that this forsakenness, which is their fault, is unforgivable. It cannot be turned around. It cannot be reversed. God will not show either of them His face again.

I Will Not Leave You Comfortless; I Will Come to You[20]

Stool Pigeon is the messenger of hope. He, like others in the Cycle, carries the spiritual and African traditions and rituals and believes that if the blood of a man or animal is spilled on the grave of Aunt Ester's dead cat, then there will be a resurrection. Aunt Ester will come back. He also believes that King has been called to greatness—that he has to go to the Top of the Mountain, to climb up. And Stool Pigeon says, God has a hand in it, and King doesn't even know it.[21] From the beginning of the play King mentions his dream in which he sees himself with a halo. It's so real that he even asks people if they can see that halo around his head.[22] No one can, of course. It is Wilson's device for alerting us to King's anointing as the one to be sacrificed, and to the play's climactic and tragic end.

Stool Pigeon, the oracle, quotes scripture completely in error, but with meaning and feeling. The details are all mixed up, but the concepts are not.

19. Ibid., 78.
20. John 14:18 (KJV).
21. *Hedley*, 64.
22. Ibid., 14.

He tells those who will listen that God's a great comforter, and he soothes pain by mentioning the lyrics of the great Negro Spiritual, "there is a Balm in Gilead." He crosses the line with some frequency when he gets carried away in speaking of God's great and awesome power and majesty, as he so often concludes with, "God's a bad motherfucker!"[23]

All of the hope and joy and possibility of a future come together in the midst of abundant tragedy when in rapid-fire succession the action begins to close. Stool Pigeon presents King with Hedley's machete, the same one with which Hedley killed Floyd, for Stool Pigeon believes that this weapon is the key to get to the Top of the Mountain. Elmore tells King, as he has promised himself he'd do, that Leroy was King's real father, and why he, Elmore, killed him.[24] King, of course, wants to redeem his actual father's honor[25] with a revenge killing of Elmore. But he has a sudden change of heart and sticks the machete into the ground where his flowers of hope are blooming. Ruby, having run into the house to get her derringer to kill Elmore for his destructive disclosure then emerges and shoots to kill Elmore, and misses. Her target instead is her son, King. She shoots her child in his throat and kills him.

King falls, bleeding on the cat's grave. Ruby is on the ground—screaming in pain for what she has just done. Stool Pigeon is ecstatic. King is sacrificed—the "fatted calf"—is sacrificed to save the others: his mother, his wife, their unborn child, Mister, Elmore, Stool Pigeon, and all the many others who would be redeemed by the renewed hope of the resurrected spirit of Aunt Ester Tyler.[26] From the sacrificial blood of one, the redemption and salvation of many. King, the Conquering Lion of Judea, the Redeemer, from

---

23. See, e.g., ibid., 28.

24. This is a flaw in the narrative. There is inadequate explanation for Elmore's determination to risk further damage to Ruby's relationship with King, by disclosing her lifelong deception of the truth of King's true father. There is some hint of a developing fatal illness in Elmore, but that is certainly an inadequate explanation for such a desperate and destructive act. Moreover, although King is clearly emotionally unbalanced by usual standards, he is not so irrational as to make such a momentary turn of allegiances away from Hedley, his assumptive father, to Leroy—a man of whom he had no knowledge that would justify a murder to avenge his death. For these reasons, *Hedley* is flawed, but they do not by any means diminish its power or its dramatic appeal.,

25. "Blood for blood, King. Be the man!" *Hedley*, 106.

26. The Crucifixion metaphor is obvious. King is "on top of the mountain," shedding the sacrificial blood to redeem and free the lives of many.

the Top of the Mountain, Our Bright and Morning Star, We Give You Our Glory.[27]

Then, as if from nowhere, the sound of a cat's meow is heard. Hope has been restored. Light has been turned on again. God and humankind are together again—the comforter and the comforted. The redeemer and the redeemed. All is right with the world. And for a brief time, peace is restored in 1985 in the Hill District of Pittsburgh, USA.

27. *Hedley*, 110.

Baltimore Center Stage 2006 Production of *Radio Golf*, with Anthony Chisholm,
John Earl Jelks, and Rocky Carroll. Photo by Richard Anderson.

CHAPTER X

All of Aunt Ester's Children Redeemed

Radio Golf

1997

UNTIL THIS FINAL PLAY August Wilson's world had focused on the African-American people who struggled to survive day-to-day in a harsh world, one that beyond the relative familiarity of the Hill District they found especially hostile. Here he would move up a few notches on the socio-economic ladder to take a close look for the first time at the black middle class.

Radio Golf[1] takes place in 1997, the sunset of the twentieth century, and many African Americans can rightfully claim their economic and political stake in America's life and future. They have been redeemed by the sufferings and the sacrifices of their ancestors. But do they remember? Do they know and understand how they got to where they are—from "tit to tat"? Do they know *who* they are? Do they hear and know the words of the God of Abraham, Isaac, and Jacob that they must remember who delivered them from slavery into freedom? Do they even know, or have they ever heard, of the embodied wisdom of Aunt Ester who teaches them how to carry the ball, and that if you drop it to go back and pick it up? Have they imbued her teachings that resentments must be set down like stony weights, and pick up tools instead—something you can use? Have they heard the blues? Do they know their song? Wilson poses these questions to the black middle class power brokers in his tenth and final play, as they are

---

1. August Wilson, *Radio Golf*, 1997.

about to raze, to obliterate, the great metaphor of their storied history and their majestic past—1839 Wylie Avenue—the ancient sanctuary of their ancestors. He completes this epic Cycle of plays with hope, for sure, for his redeemed people. Yet it is a hope tempered by doubt of their fundamental will and determination to care for one another.

Wilson started writing *Radio Golf* in 2005, and it took shape in April during rehearsal at the Yale Rep. That was fitting in that Yale was where his first serious professional theater collaborations began with Lloyd Richards on *Ma Rainey*.[2] Richards had retired by 2005. Working with his dramaturge, Todd Kreidler, the production moved to the Mark Taper in Los Angeles and then to the Seattle Repertory Company. Wilson's home was in Seattle, and his wife, Constanza Romero, was the costume designer. Wilson had to work from home. Kreidler moved in to work overnight and well into the mornings, reporting to Wilson in precise detail about the day's work with the actors, because Wilson could not leave to go to the rehearsals. He had inoperable liver cancer. Together, they constructed the play from the pieces of the material that were there, "sort of a collage."[3] I have the sense that this play was hurried—that there may have been a rush to finish before his death.[4] Perhaps there was. Death came in October 2005. He was 60.

Wilson had thought that the black middle class had lost its connection to the larger community, much of which was bereft of hope, with crime, drugs, illiteracy, and poverty. The black middle class (including leadership organizations such as the NAACP and the National Urban League), he said, should be helping with all of its skills, expertise, resources, and sophistication. He sensed that they did not feel or exercise any responsibility or duty to help, even though many had come from such communities. It was essential that the relatively well-to-do both give back and reach back to help others. There are also those African Americans—who do not have a sense of duty—of inherited means, and whose ancestors acquired wealth in businesses in black neighborhoods. The old places such as the Hill District—overrun with drugs and crime and violence—are crying out for help. *Radio Golf* is in many ways Wilson's expression of that duty.[5]

2. See the introduction and chapter III.

3. Wasikowska, "The Heartfelt Journey of Radio Golf."

4. *Radio Golf* lacks some of the rich details—the texture—of some of the earlier work, and at times feels thin. See, e.g., Brantley, "Voices Warped by the Business Blues."

5. Parks, "The Light in August."

When they had finished breakfast, Jesus said to Simon Peter, "Simon, son of John, do you love me more than these?" He said to him, "Yes, Lord; you know that I love you." Jesus said to him, "Feed my lambs."[6]

While all of the plays in the Cycle have been about struggle on the path to redemption, and often about that warrior who can and who does make horrific mistakes in battle, we could with assurance rely on the peerless beauty of language, of poetry, the discovery of song to delight the ear and soul in taking us to that place where there is reconstitution of self. Aunt Ester would show the people how to get to that place.

In *Radio Golf*, however, when candidate-for-Mayor of Pittsburgh Harmond Wilks—the well-heeled and anointed scion of the Wilks Realty family and his carefully chosen and sophisticated wife Mame, walk into the room and they speak, something is missing. The speech—the Wilson language infused with the richness of poetry, the blues, the lyricism, the lovely cadences that ease you into the play's rhythms—all of that is gone. It has been erased by assimilation. Harmond and Mame have "transcended their race," an unfortunate term that bespeaks progress for some, and a bewildering abandonment of pride and values among the more aware. It is shocking how immediately noticeable it is. It is as if someone has re-written *Hamlet* into modern English—rendering moot the need for the obligatory ten minutes to adjust to your "Shakespeare Ear." Shake your head at the aural discord. Is this August Wilson? Did he write this? What happened?

Mame is on the short list for a job with Pennsylvania's Governor. Harmond's run for Mayor is set up to be run out of the old storefront office that was once the main operation for Wilks Realty in the Hill District. It sets the right tone—shows that he has an appreciation for history. Harmond is well credentialed. He graduated from Cornell, and his business partner (and former Cornell classmate), Roosevelt Hicks, is not as polished, but dresses the part.

Then it suddenly hits: the flat dialogue and speech patterns are deliberate. They establish one side of the dramatic tension. Their language is a metaphor for their distance from the cultural heartbeat of their community, its rhythms, its pulse, the poetry, its music—the blues—the song. When Harmond and Roosevelt break out into a raucous and joyous chorus, it's not a soulful melody. Instead, it's a frat-boy-style rendition of "Hail, Hail the Gang's All Here!" The challenge for the playwright is how, when, or even if to bridge the chasm between what they have become and who they

6. John 21:15 (NRSV).

are. They are very much like Herald Loomis, who thinks (and we are told) that he is on the road in search of his wife and the mother of his child, but what becomes quite clear is that he was in search of himself—that self that got away—taken away in his case. He sought to redeem it. Harmond searches for the same.

Harmond likes history all right. He and Roosevelt, as real estate development partners are nothing more than people whose purpose is to bulldoze history. They need the Hill District declared "blighted" so that all existing structures within the designated area may be torn down, and the land cleared for apartments, a Starbucks, a Barnes and Noble, and a Whole Foods. One of the buildings is the ancient 1839 Wylie Avenue: the spiritual heart of the Hill District—a sanctuary—a Peaceful House.[7] Aunt Ester's House. To tear it down—to demolish it—is to destroy not only history but to erase the soul of the community, to rip out the heart of the African people in America, to leave them at the mercy of the enslavers in this alien land, to place them in the hands of a white Christian God—one that grows trees with no spirits in them—the same one who turned his face away as they were shackled, raped, sold, bartered, and lynched, and their families torn asunder. Oh no. That cannot happen.

Harmond does not know that yet. Roosevelt doesn't either, and won't care. Mame? Who knows? This story is about Harmond. It is about Harmond's journey. Does he find his song? Does he learn to love his people? How? How does he evolve to know the joy and love that comes from sharing what he has with them? How does his poetry return? And how is he redeemed and brought back to the wisdom and the music of his forefathers? This is the core of *Radio Golf.*

Mame, of course, wants to help Harmond get elected and is willing to help him make the right compromises to get there. She wants him to move the campaign office (with its poster-size pictures of Tiger Woods and the obligatory one of Dr. Martin Luther King, Jr.) to Shadyside where all the middle-class blacks are living. She does not want to *move back* to the Hill District, as he has suggested at times; it's a place even the TV trucks refuse to drive up to unless there has been a shooting.[8] She also tries to persuade him to change his upcoming speech, and delete the part about past police misconduct, because Harmond will need the support of the police unions. Harmond refuses. It marks the first time, among several to come, that he

7. *Gem,* 7.
8. *Radio Golf,* 8.

displays his moral compass.[9] He will come to know how to feed his people, and thus himself—that compass pointing due north.

Roosevelt Hicks only wants to get ahead, and that means more material wealth and all of the trappings. Wilson is not at all subtle here. Roosevelt loves golf, because it's a game of the rich and powerful. Golf as Wilson's metaphor for a type of freedom is clever; it is not a team sport such as that played by poor people—football, sandlot baseball, or basketball. One must have means. Ah, freedom—not for everybody—just as Roosevelt would have it. He even agrees to be the "front black face" in a radio acquisition deal in order to give a FCC minority preference to a group of white investors. Harmond is aghast, and presents Roosevelt with his honest assessment—that he's a whore and that the whole arrangement lacks personal integrity.[10]

Roosevelt has neither appreciation nor understanding of the value of history or community. He wants 1839 Wylie demolished and does not understand why anyone would question it. Harmond visits the house and describes its old-world beauty, intricate wood carvings that reveal faces and languages, beveled glass on each floor, hand carved wood balustrades, a sweet scent in the air that smells of a new day, and a sense of serenity it bestows.[11] He goes there because he discovers that his father had been paying the taxes on the house, and that his redevelopment company unwittingly obtained title to the house illegally. He went there to see if he could figure out why his father would take such interest in this house.

But Roosevelt doesn't care about the eloquent recollections of the spiritual significance of Harmond's visit, nor does he care about how questionably he and Harmond may have obtained title to the house. To him it is just some "raggedy-ass, rodent-infested, unfit-for-human-habitation eyesore that they should have torn down twenty-five years ago."[12] Roosevelt is a vandal—a greedy, self-indulgent vandal. He left the community, and in his obvious desperation to do so, he left his soul behind in the dust he kicked up getting out of there. He may be as adrift as the drug-dealers and two-bit hustlers who think they're free, while there they are—detestably—on that same treadmill, running in place.[13]

9. Ibid., 32.

10. Ibid., 80.

11. Ibid., 61. We hear Harmond's poetry here for the first time. It's as if he sings a melody of 1839 Wylie.

12. Ibid., 48.

13. Chewing the scenery. Perhaps the lack of complexity in Roosevelt's character is

Fear not, for I will redeem you;

I have singled you out by name,

You are Mine.[14]

Harmond gets visitations from two Hill District people, and finally the Wilson poetry returns. And of course, for Wilson devotees, seeing and listening to the lyricism from the slightly (or fully) eccentric characters, is like returning home again. And that is precisely what the playwright intends. His Hill District denizens have been absent in all of this redevelopment talk of money, and Starbucks, and Whole Foods. The wisdom and wispy humor have gone missing. The two who come to descend upon Harmond, each in his own way, show him back to the path—now clear—that had been the overgrown walkway to Aunt Ester's. They are messengers—these visitors, these voices and souls from his ancestral past. They will open him up to hear as he is called by name. Their appearances are indeed visitations, for they are mystical—wise and oracular—demanding close attention, for through the humor, the wackiness, the elliptical—there is truth and redemption for Harmond and for his people. Each is pure joy, and no one else writes them quite as lovely, textured, and ever revelatory like August Wilson.

Sterling is a handyman. He read about the new construction and wants some of the jobs. He is wise. He says he spent some time in jail for robbing a bank. He wanted to know what it felt like to have money. Then he realized that all you did was spend it just like everybody else. So now he would rather have something you couldn't spend over money any day. He is in stark contrast to the crass, acquisitive Roosevelt. When told that the goal is to bring back the Hill District, Sterling's reaction is that it's already dead. It can't be brought back unless Jesus is here to resurrect it.[15]

Sterling is the same Sterling from *Two Trains Running*. He redeemed Hambone's honor at his death by stealing one of Lutz's hams that Hambone had been demanding as proper recompense for labor performed. Lutz paid him with a chicken and never came through with the ham. Sterling told West, the undertaker, to place the stolen ham in Hambone's casket. Sterling here shares the story of his visit with Aunt Ester before her death. She told him that he had good understanding. He went to her because he

---

one of *Radio Golf*'s flaws. Perhaps. On the other hand, it feels good sometimes to have a clearly defined Beelzebub to attack—guiltless.

14. Isaiah 43:1 (JPS).

15. *Radio Golf*, 15.

felt sorry for himself; he was an orphan. She told him to set that down, and if he wanted to carry something to pick up a bag of tools. That is what he has been doing ever since. Her advice: "Make better what you have and you have best."[16] Aunt Ester believed in self-help and self-reliance. They are the keys to survival. They are the foundations to serenity and to peace and to salvation.

Sterling also reminds Harmond of some fundamental truths about race—about being a black man who aspires to power in a white world. He asks if he plans to be the mayor for the white people or for the black people. Harmond replies, of course, for all the people. Sterling says well the white mayors are always mayors for the white people, but when blacks get in they can't say that they want to be there for blacks. He makes an analogy to a few black students at a white school who are criticized for eating all together at lunch, yet no one says anything at all about the hundreds of white students who eat together by themselves—all the time. Finally, he warns Harmond about scoring too many points against the white man. He says if you score too many points, they will change the rules of the game on you. Here, Wilson disburses through Sterling and Harmond well-worn advice that black parents have given their sons and daughters for generations.[17] Be forewarned. The rules of the game will be changed on you when you are about to become, or are, more successful than white people. This is advice that Harmond needs to understand on his path to freedom. Roosevelt will discover it and be devastated. He will be lulled into false trust. Sterling says roughly to Roosevelt, "You holding me back. You make things hard for me. You go around kissing the white man's ass then when they see me they think I'm supposed to kiss it too . . . you ain't wanted around here."[18]

Elder Joseph Barlow or "Old Joe" was born in 1918. He is the owner of record of 1839 Wylie Avenue. He is in possession of the deed. Roosevelt sees Old Joe painting the front door and gets the police to issue him a summons for trespassing. He was painting it its traditional red color.[19] His daughter wants to move back and take possession of the house, but the house is scheduled for demolition. Harmond discovers two things. First,

16. Ibid., 54.

17. Most blacks who live and work in the White World know that the assumptions underlying that advice to be quite true.

18. *Radio Golf*, 77.

19. *Two Trains*, 24. Holloway mentions Aunt Ester for the first time. He says, "She make you right with yourself. You ain't got to go far. She live at 1839 Wylie . . . .Go up there and you'll see a red door. Go up there and knock on that."

that at the time that he and Roosevelt acquired the house for their redevelopment company, the house was not for sale. The acquisition was illegal. Second, Harmond and Old Joe are related, and Harmond's father had been paying the taxes on the house, unknown to Old Joe.

Harmond's grandfather was Caesar Wilks (from *Gem*), and Caesar's sister was Black Mary (also from *Gem*) to whom Aunt Ester must have left the house. Black Mary married *Gem's* Citizen Barlow. Together they had a son, Joseph (Old Joe) Barlow, whose daughter he named Black Mary, for his mother. Old Joe, who is quite eccentric, but charming and wise, is Harmon's cousin. Family. It explains why Harmond's father never wanted the family house to be lost to back taxes, and paid them. The result is that Harmond, along with Old Joe and Sterling, takes up the battle against Roosevelt to fight the demolition of 1839 Wylie. Aunt Ester's spirit is alive, after all, just as Stool Pigeon proclaimed.[20]

Something else more profound happens with Harmond. His speech. Recall that Wilson wrote Harmond with the flat, assimilationist-type speech pattern of the black upper-middle-class elite, presumably to highlight his, and that subgroup's, metaphorical distance from black traditions and culture and from the peoples' hearts and souls. He felt that those abandoned paid immensely, and those who climbed the ladders appeared to share no special sense of responsibility to help. That tension is played out in the dispute between Harmond and Roosevelt, and in some way between Harmond and his wife, Mame, who wants little part of that Hill District culture.

Here is an example of Harmond's internal journey to find himself—to wholeness—to redemption. In an exchange with Sterling about becoming Mayor of Pittsburgh, he says, "I'm going to be the Mayor of everybody. It's not about being black or white, it's about being American . . . .Offer [Wilson Sporting Goods] that site for a manufacturing facility right there where the steel mill was. A hundred million dollars is a powerful incentive."[21] Sterling knows he's confused.

Then after he learns of his true ancestry and his ties to Aunt Ester and to 1839 Wylie and Old Joe, Wilson's directions in the script read that, "Things have changed. He goes to his campaign poster and takes it down.

---

20. *Hedley*, 65.

21. *Radio Golf*, 57.

He looks at it a while, then shakes his head and smiles. He tears the poster in half, and throws it away.[22]

Harmon has come home. His speech to Roosevelt has all of Wilson's familiar imagery and lyricism—those that embrace his love and respect for the speaker. In his farewell to Roosevelt, he instructs him on the shifting rules for blacks in a white world. He says:

> Common sense says that ain't right. We see it different. No matter what you always on the edge. If you go to the center you look up and find everything done shifted and the center is now the edge. The rules change every day. You got to change with them. After a while the edge starts to get worn. You don't notice it at first but you're fraying with it. Oh, no, look . . . We got a black mayor. We got a black CEO. The head of our department is black. We couldn't possibly be prejudiced. Got two hundred fourteen people work in the department and two blacks but we couldn't possibly be race-conscious. Look, we even got a black football coach. You guys can sing. You can run fast. Boy, I love Nat King Cole. I love Michael Jordan. I just love him. We got a black guy works in management. Twenty-four million blacks living in poverty but it's their fault. Look, we got a black astronaut. I just love Oprah. How do you guys dance like that? After a while that center starts to give. They keep making up the rules as you go along. They keep changing the maps. Then you realize you're never going to get to that center. It's all a house of cards. Everything resting on a slim edge. Looking back you can see it all. Wasn't nothing solid about it. Everything was an *if* and a *when* and a *maybe*. Of course . . . but not really. Yes . . . but not really. I don't want to live my life like that, Roosevelt.[23]

And with this final great monologue of the Cycle, we can comfortably conclude that Harmond's song is at last in his heart and soul, that he sang his aria flawlessly and with complete control in the upper and lower registers, and with unparalleled conviction and belief in himself, and with such mountainous pride that necessitates a deep and abiding love in his creator.

Although Harmond tries to devise a plan to build around 1839 Wylie, Roosevelt opposes it and buys Harmond out in a forced sale with his white co-conspirators. Whether 1839 Wylie is or is not saved is not answered. But what we do know is that the essential reconstruction of Harmond Wilks's identity—his redemption—has surely taken place. Harmond Wilks has

22. Ibid., 74.

23. Ibid., 78–79. August Wilson's final monologue.

found his song and has reconnected to his past, his tradition, to his ancestors, and to his culture. He is known. He knows who he is. He has been called by name. Aunt Ester and all that she is, was, and will be, has called him. Harmond Wilks is standing! Harmond Wilks is shining!

Epilogue

I DRIVE OVER TO worship occasionally at Rankin Chapel on the campus at Howard University. In fact, I make a point of doing so whenever my friend, and someone whom I admire greatly, Vernon Jordan, is scheduled to preach. Soon after I had just completed my first draft of this book, I sat there among the congregants and settled in to pray, meditate, sing, and listen. As Mr. Jordan, an imposing, elegant, and impressive man stood in the pulpit, he intoned in his deep, resonant, and sonorous voice that fills every corner and niche of the space, that he was standing—standing there where once stood Dr. Mordecai Johnson, Vernon Johns, Dr. Samuel DeWitt Proctor, Dr. Gardner Taylor, Dr. Howard Thurman, and the Dr. Benjamin Mays.[1] As heads throughout nodded in assent, he called the roll. He called the roll of the ancestors. He called *on* them. He summoned them. He called them forth to empower the young black women and men of faith, of purpose and intelligence.

Jordan's message to the students is Aunt Ester's eternal message. Whatever you do, wherever you go, remember how you got to where you are. Jordan tells them on whose shoulders he stands, and they are the shoulders of the ancestors on whom they, too, stand. Without them there would be no great Howard University, and without Howard University those young women and men will not arrive at their destinations. Those ancestors and Howard are now their identity, and an integral part of who they are on their

---

1. All great African-American preachers. It is important to note that Dr. Mordecai Johnson was the first African-American President of Howard University.

journey of freedom. I wanted to shout—except he hadn't begun to preach quite yet.

It was a profound moment, and I was moved. I could hear the voice of Berniece Charles from *The Piano Lesson* as she played that piano and summoned her ancestors to come and empower the younger generation to free themselves to move forward to a new future—redeemed, fortified, and with a new vision. And I thought then that perhaps August Wilson is right. Our Christian God and our African heritage coexist in ways unique to our culture and our faith and understanding of who we are.

In a later conversation, a white Seminary President demurred. White clergy do the same thing, he said. Of course. But has it the same resonance and sense of purpose with the call to action to reach out, extend arms to pull in, reach down to pull up, and to continue the cause of liberation and redemption that a Harmond Wilks in *Radio Golf* came to comprehend? I think not. This is why the Century Cycle matters. It is an exhortation to understand that the journey is not over, and may not ever be, but still our obligation as bothers and sisters is to love one another. And our identity is embodied in our unique culture, color, tradition, and history.

Generations have been on this journey—this pilgrimage. Aunt Ester's Children. They come to see her in the sanctuary—1839 Wylie Avenue—A Peaceful House. It will remain a spiritual presence, as will she after her resurrection in *King Hedley II*, to enrich, to bless and inform. And as with her wisdom while she lived, it will be available only to those who seek it. People had to want it enough to go up to her door and knock on it, as Holloway instructs repeatedly in *Two Trains*. Harmond Wilks is struck by her spiritual presence, but only after he walks inside the house, senses its serenity, and sees its beauty. Citizen Barlow in *Gem* had to sneak in through the window, and not wait the few more days until Tuesday to see Aunt Ester and find out how his soul could be washed. Yet, until she is found, her children are rent, torn asunder by the horrors of slavery and post-Reconstruction, and then the insidious indignities, horrific humiliations, and terrors of Jim Crow and its legally enforced apartheid.

The most notable of her children are redeemed. How? They remember. They go back. Every single one finds a way of remembering how they came to be where they are. To wit: Herald Loomis in *Joe Turner* finally recalls the bones coming from the ocean with woolly hair like his, and he knows suddenly that he can stand on his own two feet and does not need anyone to sacrifice for him; the sacrifice has already been made by his own people, and he can bleed for himself.

This is the Exodus story on which Wilson relies. Remember who liberated you with an outstretched arm and a mighty hand. Wilson tells his people to remember the Emancipation—our Passover; our Exodus; our Deliverance—as *Hedley's* Stool Pigeon says, "how we got from tit to tat." Stop, pause, remember. Know how, who, what, when, such that we can know our ancestors—our freedom fighters—our redeemers. Without conscience the enslavers shredded our families for profit. Our mothers and sisters were bred, sold, and purchased for their capacity to increase, and were raped repeatedly for the purpose. Their children were lawfully not theirs, and were sold off away from them. Yet after emancipation many of us were able to reconstitute ourselves, re-gather as much of our families as possible, and become whole. To know our identities. A reconstituted personality who can sing a song to affirm a new life. This is August Wilson's gift of language. This is his gift of drama. It is his gift of poetry.

He also asks the rather discomfiting question of how do the enslaved worship and come to love the same God of the enslaver? He says that when you look in the mirror you should be able to see a God that looks like you. There is frequent tension between the worship of the Christian God and the worship of the God (gods?) of the mystical, the metaphysical, the spectral worlds brought from Africa.[2] Sometimes that tension is explosive and offensive; sometimes the Christian God is rejected, even cursed or blasphemed. But more commonly, on redemption's road Aunt Ester's children inhabit the same world as she does—a world in which Christianity and the African are coexistent, mutually enriching and fully embracing of a loving and merciful God. And in Wilson's Century Cycle, it is that God who loves the people just as they as are, and who has them hear the message of liberation never intended or ever conceived of by the enslaver.

Wilson scholars have never fully developed an analysis of his father-son relationships in the Cycle. Even when the fathers are not present they

2. There is a common African belief that gods inhabit material objects, and such beliefs found their way into traditional African-American Christian ritual. See, e.g., Raboteau, *Slave Religion: The "Invisible Institution" in the Antebellum South*, 33. Also, a slave cabin found on Edisto Island, South Carolina, and to be on display in the Smithsonian National Museum of African American History and Culture, is painted a pale blue and thought to be the original paint. It was pale blue because the Yoruban tribal belief was that the blue kept evil spirits away. There were devout African-American Christians on Edisto Island.

seem to have a profound effect on their sons and their decisions and their capacity to make decisions. Levee in *Ma Rainey* seeks to avenge his father's lynching; Boy Willie in *The Piano Lesson* may have slain in revenge for his father's murder. Hedley's legacy in *Seven Guitars* and its fundamental dishonesty completely thwart the next generation; Troy Maxson in *Fences* comes perilously close to destroying his son, Cory, as does Becker his son Booster in *Jitney*. Harmond barely manages to escape his father's controlling memory in *Radio Golf*. This eternal Oedipal struggle has gone completely unexamined and is quite ripe for close inspection, especially through a theological lens.

I do not by any measure believe that August Wilson set out to write these plays with the notion of raising theological questions. I suppose he might have been slightly intrigued by my inquiry, maybe even amused. There is no doubt, however, that theological issues are present and beautifully explored, intended or not. All literature takes on a life of its own, distinct from the intention of the creator,[3] and becomes a new creation in the mind of each reader. And thus have I taken such liberties with the Century Cycle. I have enjoyed this walk with August Wilson—far exceeding already high expectations—and it continues to give more. To the discerning reader and theatergoer, he is not necessarily an easy read nor is he a light and frothy entertaining evening of theater. Oh I suppose one can go and merely be entertained by the plot—walking out to the car, recalling what happened. His work requires the interrogation, "What did this mean? What was its significance?" My goal has been to assist in both framing the questions and suggesting some responses.

This exploration has at times taken on a sense that Wilson created a patchwork of images—a storefront here, a backyard there, a commercial strip punctuated by residences in need of repair yet still capable of providing amply for the shelter, sustenance, and protection that only the Divine can give. Those images are much like the Bearden collages that he admired, and that inspired his literary and dramatic vision.

There is also the patchwork of speeches—I call them songs—that are not just spoken, but settle into the soul and on the ear as sublime as the voice of Sarah Vaughan in mid-range, or as smooth as the dulcet tones that were Billy Eckstine's. And then those scenes of such operatic power—Troy Maxson singing to explain why he needed to leave Rose's bed—to go beyond the fence ["I come in here every day with a sack of potatoes and a

---

3. See, e.g., the Ralph Ellison *Invisible Man* lesson, as discussed in the introduction.

bucket of lard . . . I give you the lint from my pockets."] and Rose's aria when she sings that when she wanted to stray she just held on tighter. It's the blues—and a determination to go on living, no matter what. Each play, in varying textures and layers is its own salvation story. Collectively, the Century Cycle stands as a powerful witness to August Wilson's faith in the resiliency of the spirit that is black America—Aunt Ester's children—weary, but still on that road.

Bibliography

Baldwin, James. *The Fire Next Time*. New York: Dell, 1962.

Baptist, Edward E. *The Half Has Never Been Told: Slavery and the Making of American Capitalism*. New York: Basic, 2014.

Baraka, Amiri. "Improvisation on *Wise, Why's, Y's* (excerpts from Africa Section)." In *Fooling with Words with Bill Moyers: The Poets Read*. Online: http://billmoyers.com/content/fooling-with-words-part-i/.

Bigsby, Christopher. "An Interview with August Wilson, 1991." In *The Cambridge Companion to August Wilson*, edited by Christopher Bigsby, 202–13. Cambridge: Cambridge University Press, 2007.

———. "August Wilson: The Ground on Which He Stood. " In *The Cambridge Companion to August Wilson*, edited by Christopher Bigsby, 1–27. Cambridge: Cambridge University Press, 2007.

Blackmon, Douglas A. *Slavery by Another Name: The Re-Enslavement of Black Americans from the Civil War to World War II*. New York: Anchor, 2008.

Bogumil, Mary L. "August Wilson's Relationship to Black Theatre: Community, Aesthetics, History and Race." In *The Cambridge Companion to August Wilson*, edited by Christopher Bigsby, 52–64. Cambridge: Cambridge University Press, 2007.

Booker, Margaret. "Radio Golf: The Courage of His Convictions – Survival, Success, and Spirituality." In *The Cambridge Companion to August Wilson*, edited by Christopher Bigsby, 183–92. Cambridge: Cambridge University Press, 2007.

Bottoms, Stephen. "Two Trains Running: Blood on the Tracks." In *The Cambridge Companion to August Wilson*, edited by Christopher Bigsby, 145–57. Cambridge: Cambridge University Press, 2007.

Boyd, Herbert. "Interview with August Wilson, 2000." In *Conversations with August Wilson*, edited by Jackson R. Bryer and Mary C. Hartig, 235–40. Jackson: University of Mississippi Press, 2006.

Branch, Taylor. *Parting the Waters: America in the King Years 1954–63*. New York: Simon and Schuster, 1988.

———. *Pillar of Fire: America in the King Years 1963–65*. New York: Simon and Schuster, 1998.

———. *At Canaan's Edge: America in the King Years 1965–68*. New York: Simon and Schuster, 2006.

Brantley, Ben. "Voices Warped by the Business Blues." *New York Times* (April 30, 2005) E1.

———. "In a Diner, Chewing the Fat and Burying the Dead." *New York Times* (December 4, 2006) E1.

Butler, Jon. *Awash in a Sea of Faith: Christianizing the American People*. Cambridge: Harvard University Press, 1990.

Carter, Anthony J. *On Being Black and Reformed*. Phillipsburg: P&R, 1979.

Cone, James H. *A Black Theology of Liberation*. New York: Orbis, 1986

———. *For My People: Black Theology and the Black Church*. New York: Orbis 1984.

———. *The Spirituals and the Blues: An Interpretation*. New York, Orbis, 1972.

Dezell, Maureen. "The 10-Play Odyssey Continues with *Gem of the Ocean, 2004*." In *Conversations with August Wilson,* edited by Jackson R. Bryer and Mary C. Hartig, 253–56. Jackson: University of Mississippi Press, 2006.

Elam, Harry J., Jr. "August Wilson's Women." In *May All Your Fences Have Gates: Essays on the Drama of August Wilson,* edited by Alan Nadel, 165–82. Iowa City: University of Iowa Press, 1994.

———. "*Gem of the Ocean* and the Redemptive Power of History." In *The Cambridge Companion to August Wilson,* edited by Christopher Bigsby, 75–88. Cambridge: Cambridge University Press, 2007.

Evans, James H. *We Have Been Believers: An African American Systematic Theology*. Minneapolis: Augsborg Fortress, 1992.

Feingold, Michael. "August Wilson's Bottomless Blackness, 1984." In *Conversations with August Wilson,* edited by Jackson R. Bryer and Mary C. Hartig, 12–18. Jackson: University of Mississippi Press, 2006.

Fishman, Joan. "Romare Bearden, August Wilson, and the Traditions of African Performance." In *May All Your Fences Have Gates: Essays on the Drama of August Wilson,* edited by Alan Nadel, 133–49. Iowa City: University of Iowa Press, 1994.

Fleche, Anne. "The History Lesson: Authenticity and Anachronism in August Wilson's Plays." In *May All Your Fences Have Gates: Essays on the Drama of August Wilson,* edited by Alan Nadel, 9–20. Iowa City: University of Iowa Press, 1994

Gates, Henry Louis, Jr. and Donald Yacovone. *The African Americans: Many Rivers to Cross*. New York: SmileyBooks, 2013.

Gomes, Peter J. *Strength for the Journey: Biblical Wisdom for Daily Living*. New York: HarperCollins, 2003.

Grant, Nathan L. "Men, Women and Culture: A Conversation with August Wilson, 1993." In *Conversations with August Wilson,* edited by Jackson R. Bryer and Mary C. Hartig, 172–87. Jackson: University of Mississippi Press, 2006.

Hay, Samuel A. "*Joe Turner's Come and Gone*." In *The Cambridge Companion to August Wilson,* edited by Christopher Bigsby, 89–101. Cambridge: University of Cambridge Press, 2007.

Heard, Elisabeth J. "August Wilson on Playwriting: An Interview, 1999." In *Conversations with August Wilson,* edited by Jackson R. Bryer and Mary C. Hartig, 223–34. Jackson: University of Mississippi Press, 2006.

Herrington, Joan. "*King Hedley II*: In the Midst of All This Death." In *The Cambridge Companion to August Wilson,* edited by Christopher Bigsby, 169–82. Cambridge: University of Cambridge Press, 2007.

Hughes, Langston. *The Collected Poems of Langston Hughes,* edited by Arnold Rampersad. New York: Alfred A. Knopf, 1994.

Isherwood, Charles. "At War With Ghosts of History." *New York Times* (March 12, 2007) E1.

———. "August Wilson, Theater's Poet of Black America, is Dead at 60." *New York Times* (October 3, 2005) A1.

Johnson, James Weldon, and J. Rosamond Johnson. *The Books of American Negro Spirituals.* New York: Viking, 1926.

Krasner, David. "*Jitney*: Folklore and Responsibility." In *The Cambridge Companion to August Wilson,* edited by Christopher Bigsby, 158–68. Cambridge: University of Cambridge Press, 2007.

Kreidler, Todd. Dramaturge to August Wilson. On-going conversations during the research and writing in 2012 and 2013.

Lahr, John. "Been Here and Gone." *The New Yorker,* April 16, 2001.

Levine, Lawrence W. *Black Culture and Black Consciousness: Afro-American Folk Thought from Slavery to Freedom.* New York: Oxford University Press, 2007.

Londre, Felicia Hardison. "A Piano and its History: Family and Transcending Family." In *The Cambridge Companion to August Wilson,* edited by Christopher Bigsby, 113–23. Cambridge: University of Cambridge Press, 2007.

Lyons, Bonnie. "An Interview with August Wilson: 1997." In *Conversations with August Wilson,* edited by Jackson R. Bryer and Mary C. Hartig, 204–22. Jackson: University of Mississippi Press, 2006.

Mbiti, John S. *Introduction to African Religion.* Oxford: Heinemann, 1991.

Moyers, Bill. "August Wilson: Playwright," In *Bill Moyers: A World of Ideas – Conversations with Thoughtful Men and Women About American Life and the Ideas Shaping Our Future,* 167–80. New York: Doubleday, 1989.

Murphy, Brenda. "The Tragedy of *Seven Guitars.*" In *The Cambridge Companion to August Wilson,* edited by Christopher Bigsby, 124–34. Cambridge: Cambridge University Press, 2007.

Parks, Suzan-Lori. "The Light in August." *American Theatre* 22 (November 2005) 22–25, 74–78.

Pettengill, Richard. "The Historical Perspective: An Interview with August Wilson 1993." In *Conversations with August Wilson,* edited by Jackson R. Bryer and Mary C. Hartig, 155–71. Jackson: University of Mississippi Press, 2006.

Plimpton, George. "August Wilson: The Art of Theater." *The Paris Review* 153 (Winter 1999). Online: http://www.theparisreview.org/interviews/839/august-wilson-the-art-of-theater-no-14-august-wilson.

Powers, Kim. "An Interview with August Wilson." In *Conversations with August Wilson,* edited by Jackson R. Bryer and Mary C. Hartig, 3–11. Jackson: University of Mississippi Press, 2006

Rashad, Phylicia. "Foreword." In August Wilson, *Gem of the Ocean,* xxvii–xxxi. New York: Theatre Communications Group, 2007

Raboteau, Albert J. *Slave Religion: The 'Invisible Institution' in the Antebellum South.* Oxford: Oxford University Press, 2004.

Rahner, Karl. *The Trinity.* New York: Crossroad, 2010.

Rich, Frank. "Foreword." In *Ma Rainey's Black Bottom,* by August Wilson. New York: Theatre Communications Group, 2007.

Savran, David. "August Wilson 1987." In *Conversations with August Wilson*, edited by Jackson R. Bryer and Mary C. Hartig, 19–37. Jackson: University of Mississippi Press, 2006.

Shannon, Sandra G., and Dana A. Williams. "A Conversation with August Wilson, 2003." In *Conversations with August Wilson*, edited by Jackson R. Bryer and Mary C. Hartig, 241–52. Jackson: University of Mississippi Press, 2006.

Sheppard, Vera. "August Wilson: An Interview, 1990." In *Conversations with August Wilson*, edited by Jackson R. Bryer and Mary C. Hartig, 101–17. Jackson: University of Mississippi Press, 2006.

Spangler, Jewel L. *Virginians Reborn: Anglican Monopoly, Evangelical Dissent, and the Rise of the Baptists in the Late Eighteenth Century*. Charlottesville: University of Virginia Press, 2008.

Walker, Margaret. *This is My Century: New and Collected Poems*. Athens: University of Georgia Press, 1989.

Wasikowska, Mia. "The Heartfelt Journey of Radio Golf," *New York Times* (May 7, 2007) E1.

Watlington, Dennis. "Hurdling Fences." *Vanity Fair* 52 (April 1989) 102–13.

Wilkerson, Isabel. *The Warmth of Other Suns: The Epic Story of America's Great Migration*. New York: Random House, 2010.

Williams, Tennessee. *A Streetcar Named Desire*. New York: Penguin, 1947.

Wilson, August. "Aunt Ester's Children: A Century on Stage." *American Theatre* 22 (November 2005) 26–30.

———. *Fences*. 1957. New York: Theatre Communications Group, 2007.

———. *Gem of the Ocean*. 1904. New York: Theatre Communications Group, 2007.

———. *The Ground On Which I Stand*. New York: Theatre Communications Group, 1996.

———. *How I Learned What I Learned*. Co-conceived with Todd Kreidler, a play Produced and Performed by August Wilson in 2003 for the Seattle Repertory Company, and Produced in October 2014 by the Kenny Leon's True Colors Theatre Company, Atlanta, Directed by Todd Kreidler and Performed by Eugene Lee.

———. "I Want A Black Director." *New York Times* (September 26, 1990) A25.

———. *Jitney*. 1977. New York: Theatre Communications Group, 2007.

———. *Joe Turner's Come and Gone*. 1911. New York: Theatre Communications Group, 2007.

———. *King Hedley II*. 1985. New York: Theatre Communications Group, 2007.

———. *Ma Rainey's Black Bottom*. 1927. New York: Theatre Communications Group, 2007.

———. *The Piano Lesson*. 1936. New York: Theatre Communications Group, 2007.

———. *Radio Golf*. 1997. New York: Theatre Communications Group, 2007.

———. Foreword. Schwartzman, Myron. *Romare Bearden: His Life and Art*. New York: Harry N. Abrams, 1997.

———. *Seven Guitars*. 1948. New York: Theatre Communications Group, 2007.

———. *Two Trains Running*. 1969. New York: Theatre Communications Group, 2007.

Zizioulas, John D. *Being As Communion: Studies in Personhood and the Church*. New York: SVS, 1985.

Acknowledgments

THIS BOOK IS DEDICATED to the memory of my father, David L. Temple Sr. (1911–1995), who was always, and without fail, my steadfast support in every way. And to the memory of my mother, Helen (1919–2000), for inspiring me with the love of theater, the written and spoken word, and the beauty of language. And a special dedication to the memory of my much-too-soon tragically departed friend, Edwin C. Gardner (1950–1992), who introduced me to Washington's Arena Stage in 1971. The result has been a collaboration of decades that nourishes my spirit in ways yet unfolding.

My seminary Hebrew Scriptures Professor, the Rev. Dr. Judy Fentress-Williams, is a brilliant scholar, thesis advisor, teacher, mentor, confidant, critic, and dear friend. She guided me through this with a deep and abiding respect for my own knowledge and desire for further inquiry. It was a wondrous collaboration for which I am truly grateful.

To Virginia Seminary's President and Dean, the Very Rev. Ian Markham, I extend warmest regards and thanks for introducing me to this publisher with such lovely praise.

And to Kenny Leon and to Todd Kreidler, August Wilson's director of choice and dramaturge, respectively, whose friendships and support throughout the years have been inspiring, and whose unique collaborations with the playwright gave me invaluable insight always. Thank you, Kenny, and to Todd, my dear friends.

Finally, I extend sincere gratitude to my editor, Charlie Collier, for his special promotion, wisdom, and assistance. There are others who graciously assisted in the production: Richard Anderson, Christopher Farmer, Greta Hays, Colin Hovde, Alison Irvin, Kevin Maroney, Molly Smith, Jordan Stepp, Scott Suchman, and Zoe Wilson.

WITHDRAWN

CPSIA information can be obtained
at www.ICGtesting.com
Printed in the USA
LVOW08s0055260517

535910LV00001B/135/P